What raging fire shall flood the soul?

What rich desire unlocks its door?

What sweet seduction lies before us?

Past the point of no return, the final threshold

What warm unspoken secrets will we learn?

From Phantom of the Opera,
Past the Point of No Return

Other books by Julia Trops

Art and Money (Tentative title) coming soon
2012 Okanagan Erotic Art Show Catalog
2011 Okanagan Erotic Art Show Catalog
Simplicity in Mind - catalog for the Livessence Society for Figurative Artists and Models
2009 Okanagan Erotic Art Show Catalog
Lauren - Sensuality of Form

unSpoken Secrets

2013 Okanagan Erotic Art Show Catalog

hosted by Sparkling Hill Resort
5 July - 2 August 2013

http://www.OkanaganEroticArtShow.com
http://www.Facebook.com/EroticArtShow

Published by Julia Trops ISBN 978-0-9813363-4-3

Cover artwork titled "Dripping Desire" used with permission by Margot
Artwork photo courtesy of Eric Simard (model Hailey Winkelaar)
Photograph of Gary Mitchell by Michelle Waters, all rights reserved
Photograph of Annemarie Fux by Christian Reiner
Photographs and copy provided by and are the property of Sparkling Hill Resort

Font: title page: Treasure Map Deadhand by GemFonts
Paragraphs: Adobe Garamond Pro

This book is dedicated to the artists in this catalog. Thank you for putting on a great show:

Aarron Laidig, Alexandra Edmonds, Annemarie Fux, April Bosshard, Brenda Maunders,
Calvin Bradbury, Carrie Harper, Catherine Dalfort, Christine Allan, Cynthia Gibson, Dan McCormack,
Daniel McKellar, Debby Merkel, Deborah Rehm, Dirk Hiel, Edward Vincent, Elizabeth Kozlowski,
Foster Gauley, Gary Mitchell, Gracie Ackerman, Greg Riley, Jacqueline Grosser, Jaine Buse,
James Postill, Jan Dawson, Jan Little, Jennifer Burrows, Jessika LaFramboise, Johann Wessels,
Julie-Ann Miller, June Seed, Keith Funk, Kena Cumming Cormier, Kendi Clearwater,
Kim-Alan Dawson, Kim Walker, Krista Berrigan, Kristine Lee, Laurel Fredin, Lawrence Cormier,
Linda Franklin, Lisa Figueroa, Lynn Erin, Margot, Mario Vucinovec, Marissa Brown & Avery De Rousie
Michelle Stephenson, Nicholas Vincent, Nina Kuriloff, Pat DeLuca, Peggy Stel, Robert Canaga,
Robert Simkins, Robyn Gold, Ron West, Rory O'Neill, Roxi Sim Hermsen, Ryan Robson,
Sarah Parsons, Shannon Holand, Sharon Lancaster, Sharon Rose, Shaz, Suzanne LeStage, Tina Siddiqui
Trina Ganson, Una Connor, Chad Henderson, Victoria Pendragon, Victoria Skofteby

To my fellow jurors Nick Bantock and Paul Crawford, thank you!

To Hans-Peter Mayr, General Manager and CEO, for suggesting the show be hosted at Sparkling Hill,
and being such a terrific art supporter!

To Sharon Lancaster for being such a great Submissions Assistant,
To Jennifer Burrows who has consistently and generously helped out with time and interest,
To my beautiful daughters, Miranda and Kim, and my wonderful son Aaron,
for being the best ticketing persons ever,

But most importantly, to my husband Chris and best friend and supporter, I love you!

Preface

The Okanagan Erotic Show emerged in 2007, fellow artists Lauren Wilson, Angela Hansen and myself were talking about having an art show that was a bit more exciting than the usual run of the mill life drawing exhibitions. We were having a sip (or two, maybe more, I can't remember) of wine while manning the Livessence booth at one of the local art shows, and noticed there were many people who would barely glance at the nudes on display. Censorship about what was "proper" had reared its ugly head. Knowing full well that erotic is perceived individually, we wanted to shake things up. We wanted to have some FUN!

The first show, "Blush, what makes you?" at the Rotary Centre for the Arts (RCA) in 2008 was a huge success, but as you can imagine, as the RCA is a public building, there were a few complaints. In 2009, Angela went on to have her first child, and Lauren went traveling in Asia, so that year, I carried on my own, and have since. "Raw......Whispers" was at A. Woodside Design Gallery, and that year I created the first catalog. I realized how important that record seemed to be to each artist and I had fun doing it.

2010 saw a bit of rough bumps and grinds, but that experience showed me where we, the Okanagan artists, were in terms of comfort level and where we, the local public, were in terms of artistic support and adventure. "Seduce Me" (2010), "The Edge of Night" (2011) and "Rumour has it..." (2012) were held at a new winery, Ex Nihilo Vineyards in Lake Country. I was overwhelmed by the attendance at the opening nights, and the tremendously positive comments on the show throughout its run. Each year it increased in popularity and attendance with 300 attendees in 2012 at opening night, and many of the artists, and patrons, dressed up!

The charity chosen for 2012 and 2013 is the Central Okanagan Hospice Association, in memory of Tracie Ward, the Executive Director of the Rotary Centre for the Arts from 2005 - 2012. Tracie was the first champion of the first Erotic Show in spite of the negative comments received, her view was that the RCA is an Arts Centre first and foremost. Thank you Tracie!

At the 2012 Opening Night, I was approached by Hans-Peter Mayr, General Manager and CEO of Sparkling Hills Resort, who indicated he would be interested in presenting the show. 2013 sees a new venue, a quite exciting Opening Night planned, and as you will see, a new level reached! Hope you enjoy!

Introduction

The erotic does not end in spastic contractions and reflex discharges;
it transcends them, to reach into the ethereal realms of memory and feeling,
*like a note that reverberates long after the string has pulsated.**

I think the world's best loved creations are erotic. Consider Phantom of the Opera and Cats, melodies and concerts like Tchaikovsky's Nutcracker Suite, or movies like The African Queen or 2001: A Space Odyssey. These creations tease you, they suggest, the present, they provide longing and desire, they reach down in to our very soul and pull and push and grip to that essence of being human, of being alive.

Critics describe electricity being in the air when certain performers step on stage, and it is the same for artwork, or for dance or for music. That electricity is a symbiotic relationship between the artist and the patron, teasing, engaging the viewer, by encouraging curiosity, butterfly wings, soft and gentle against the cheek, or by providing a metaphoric dark corridor where they can wander down and discover themselves through the artist's creative act. Erotic and evocative, presentation and response, the artist, regardless if actor, musician, or painter, we all hope for that connection to be sparkling and electric, alive with caresses and whispers, seducing your attention, stroking the emotional funnybone. I know I REALLY like my funny bone stroked, how bout you?

As you can see, I do not subscribe to the standard definition of erotic being related strictly to physical sex, or physical sexual arousal. The Opening Night is a mixture of this sensuality: visual and auditory, with Sparkling Hill's scrumptious appetizers, all to provoke you, intrigue you, add mystery and create wonderful memories, accessible long after the night has ended.

F. Gonzalez-Crussi, Mexican-born U.S. pathologist, educator. "The Conditions for Seduction, According to an Old Chinese Text," On the Nature of Things Erotic, Harcourt Brace (1988).

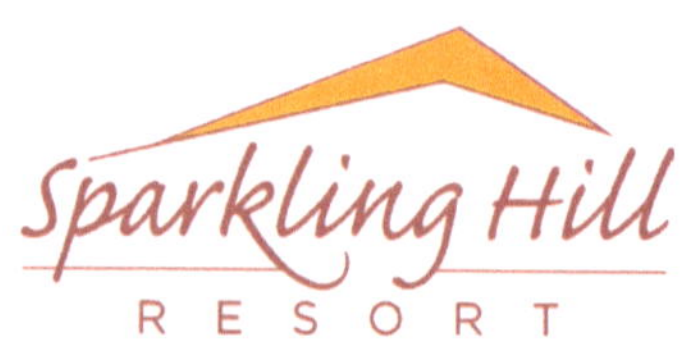

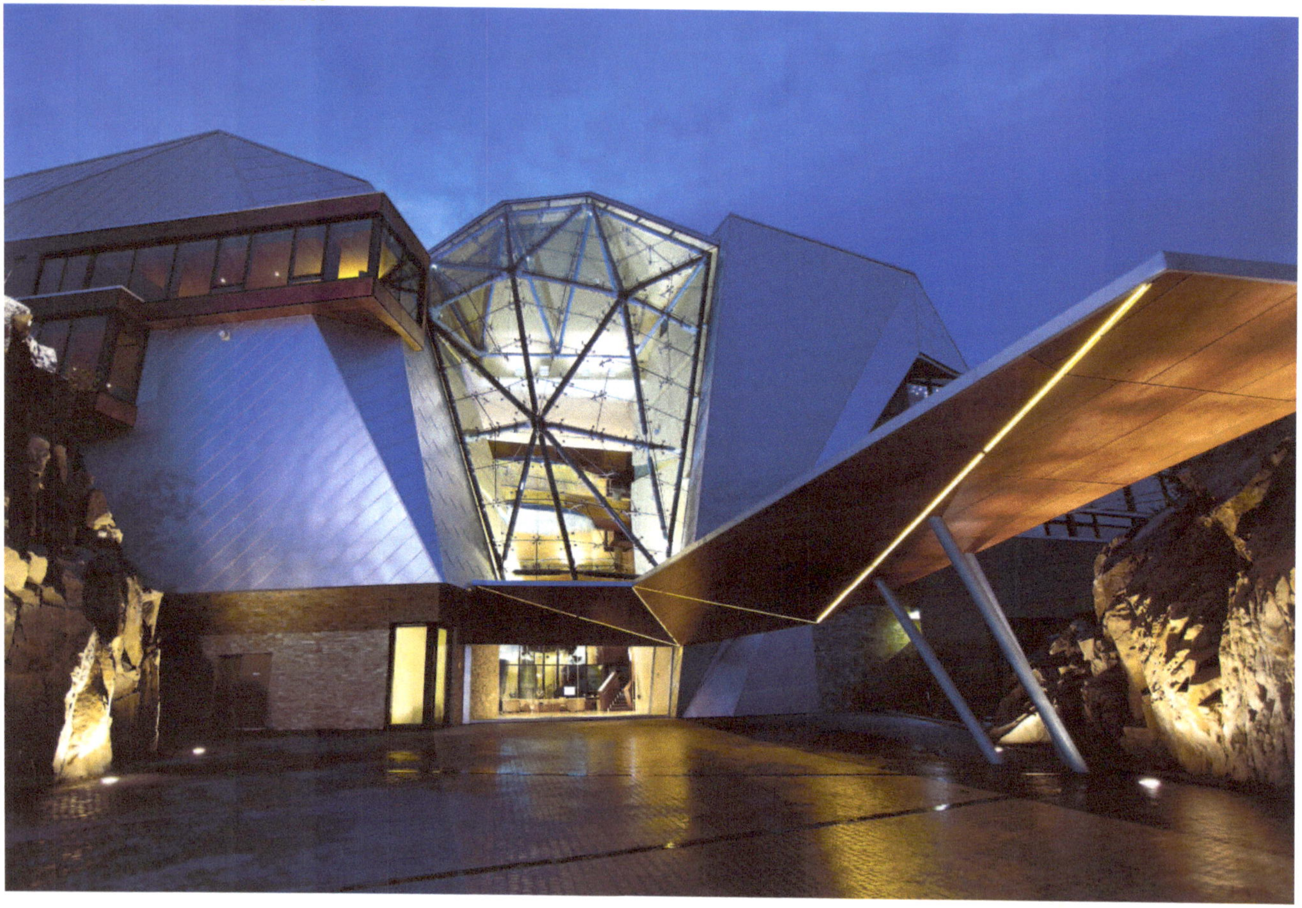

Sparkling Hill Resort
888 Sparkling Place
Vernon, BC V1H 2K7
www.SparklingHill.com
Reservations@SparklingHill.com or 1.877.275.1556

Sparkling Hill Resort is a 149-room European inspired destination wellness hotel, owned by Mr. Gernot Langes Swarovski, patriarch of the Swarovski crystal dynasty.

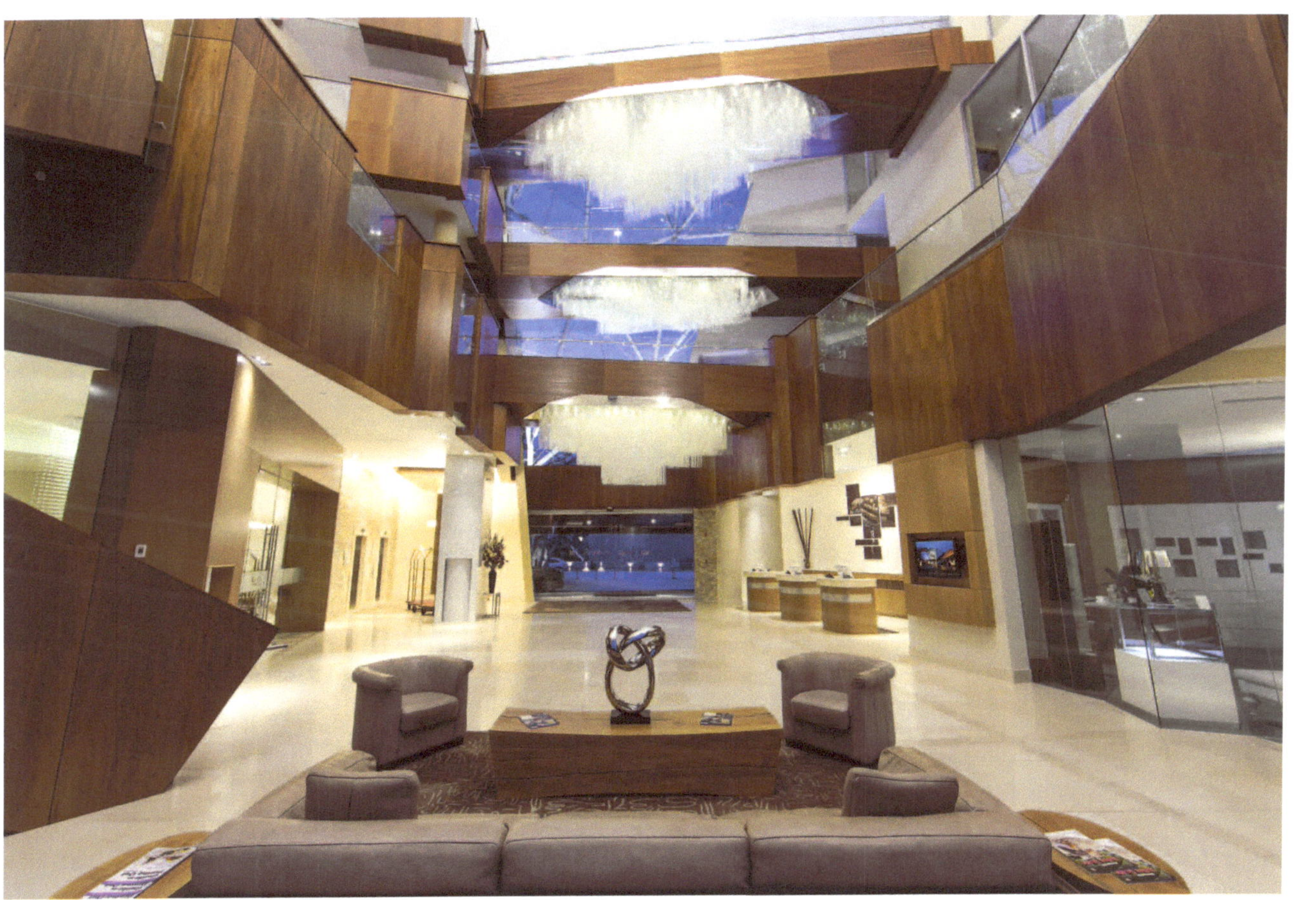

The resort, opened in the summer of 2010, combines the elegance of dazzling Swarovski crystal elements with the natural splendor of the Okanagan. Situated on the apex of a granite ridge, high above the famed Predator Ridge Golf Resort, Sparkling Hill offers guests not only spectacular views of the surrounding mountains, golf course and Lake Okanagan but is a quiet respite to rejuvenate & reenergize. It is the first hotel in North America to incorporate 3.5 million Swarovski crystal elements into every aspect of its design and structure.

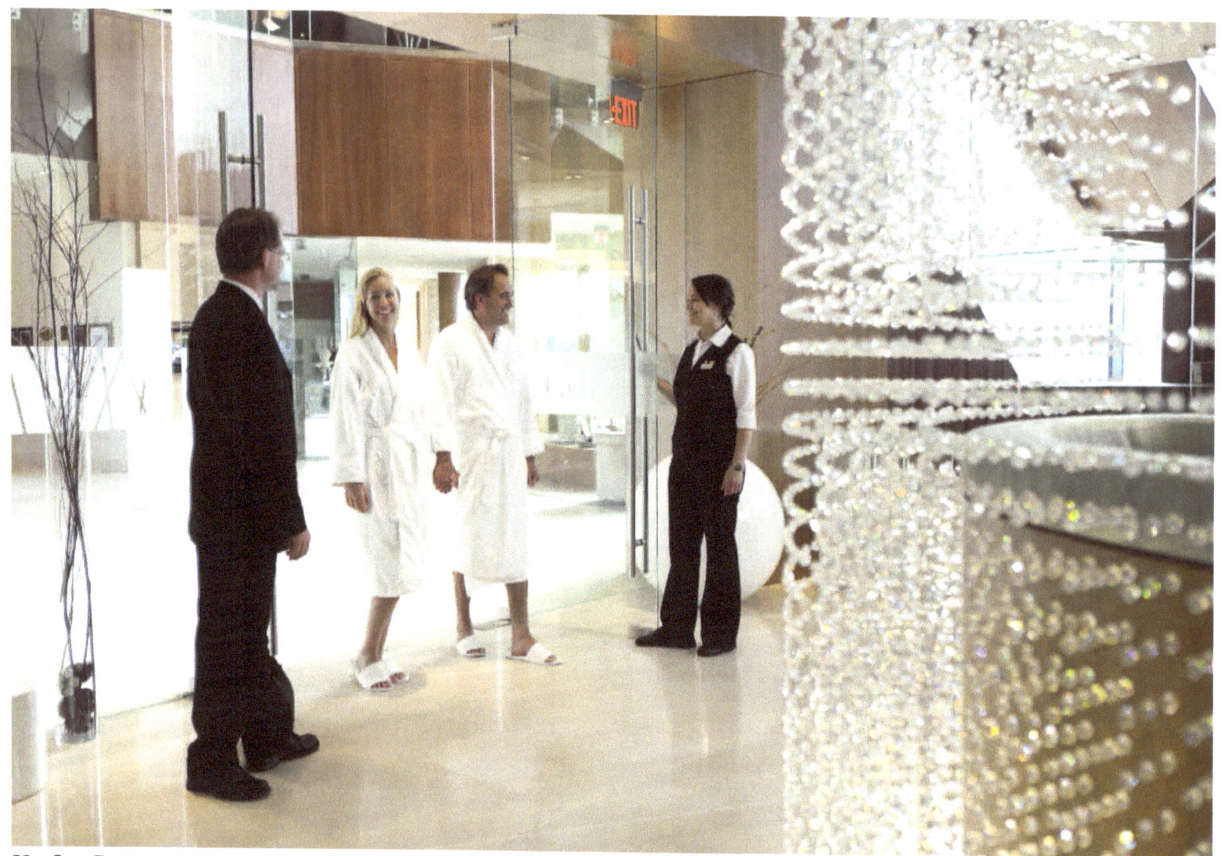

KurSpa Reception

The 40 thousand sq ft KurSpa is the largest in Canada, it incorporates 48 treatment rooms, seven steam and sauna rooms, aqua mediation, Serenity and Tea Relaxation Rooms, Kneipp water therapy pool, outdoor infinity pool and indoor pool.

The KurSpa offers over 100 treatments, many that go beyond traditional spa experiences and conventional pampering. One of these treatments is the Cryotherapy Cold Sauna, the first in North America. Set at a bone chilling (-110°C / -166°F) it is used for the treatment of arthritis and sports injury recovery.

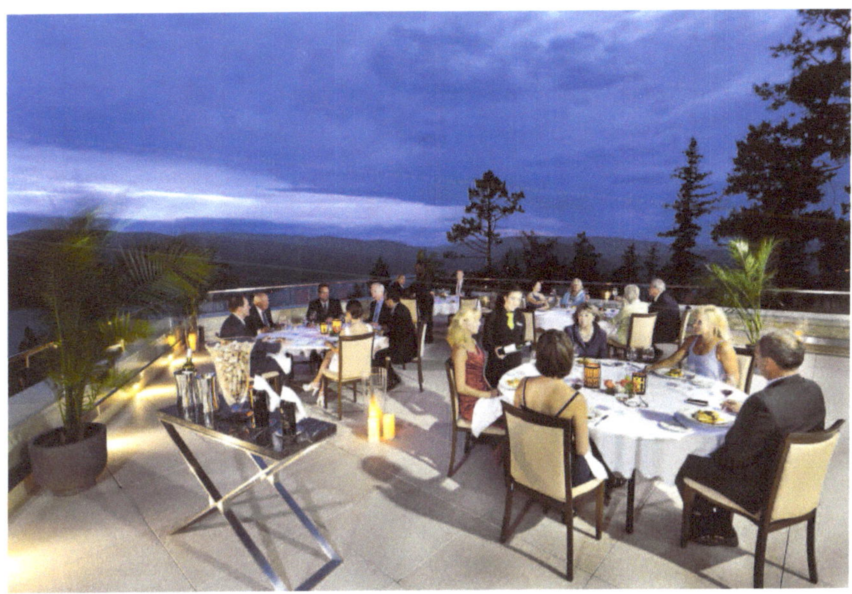
Outdoor Terrace Dining

Fine dining in PeakFine or casual social dining in Barrique Java offers expansive views of mountains and lake.

Located a scenic 25-minute drive north from the Kelowna International Airport. The area attracts golf, ski, hiking, boating and wine enthusiasts to the four season play ground of the Okanagan Valley.

Sparkling Hill is an exceptional resort in an exceptional destination.

Hans-Peter Mayr, CEO of Sparkling Hill Resort is enthusiastic about hosting the Erotic Art Show; he says "Sparkling Hill Resort is delighted to be part of this exciting opportunity.

We are very supportive of local artists and community and are happy to get involved with this project. We look forward to exhibiting some of the spectacular pieces of art throughout the resort this summer."

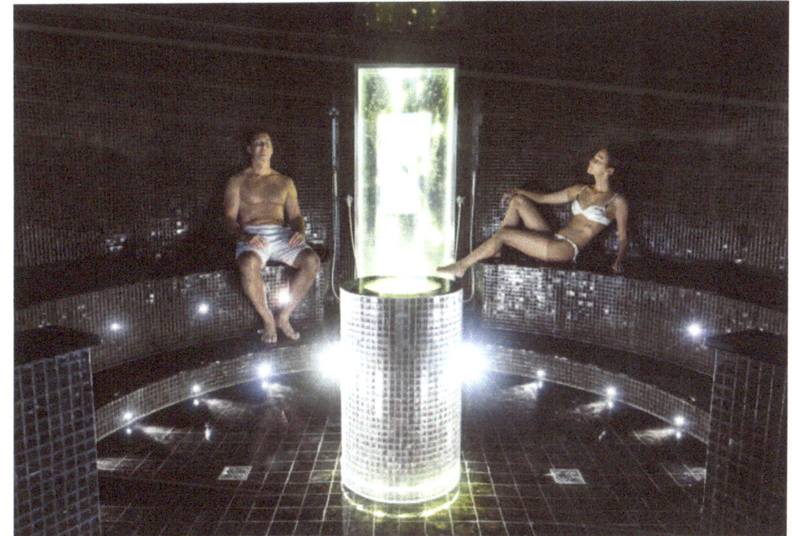
Crystal Steam

The Jurors

Jurying was blind.
No names were included with the artwork.
The jury had three ways in to the artwork - the visual, the title, and the artist statement.

Nick Bantock

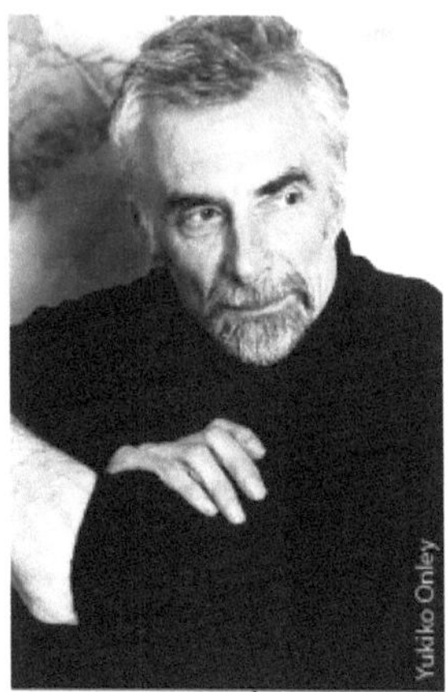

Nick was schooled in England and has a BA in Fine Art (painting). He has authored 25 books, 11 of which have appeared on the best seller lists, including 3 books on the New York Times top ten at one time. 'Griffin and Sabine' stayed on that list for over two years. His works have been translated into 13 languages and over 5 million have been sold worldwide.

Once named by the classic SF magazine Weird Tales as one of the best 85 storytellers of the century. He has written articles and stories for numerous international newspapers and magazine's. His Wasnick blogs are much followed on Facebook and Twitter. His paintings, drawings, sculptures, collages and prints have been exhibited in shows in UK, France and North America.

In 2010 Nick's major retrospective exhibition opened at the MOA in Denver. His works are in private collections throughout the world. Nick has a lifetime BAFTA (British Oscar) for CD Rom 'Ceremony of Innocence', created with Peter Gabriel's Real World. Ceremony (soundtrack by Isabella Rossolini and Ben Kingsley). He has two ipad apps, 'Sage' and 'The Venetian' and is working on a third. Three of his books have been optioned for film and his stage play based on the 'Griffin and Sabine' double trilogy premiered in Vancouver 2006.

Produced artwork for over 300 book covers (including works by Roth and Updike), illustrated Viking Penguin's new translation of Chaucer's 'Canterbury Tales'. He's designed theater posters for the London plays of Tom Stoppard and Alec Guinness.

For 20 years he's spoken and read to audiences throughout North America, Europe and Australia. Given keynote and motivational speeches to corporations and teachers state conferences. He's given dramatic readings on the radio and the stage and has been interviewed (way too many times) for TV, radio and print.

He's worked in a betting shop in the East End of London, trained as a psychotherapist, designed and had built a house that combined an Indonesian temple and a Russian orthodox church with an English cricket pavilion and a New Orleans bordello.

Between 2007 and 2010 was one of the twelve committee members responsible for selecting Canada's postage stamps.

Among the things he can't do: Can't swim, never ridden a horse, his spelling is dreadful and his singing voice is flat as a pancake.

www.NickBantock.com
Nick-Bantock.blogspot.ca/
www.NickBantock.com/workshops.php

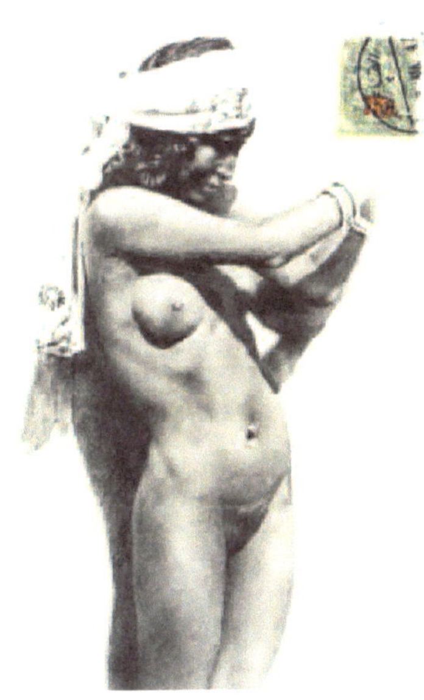

Paul Crawford

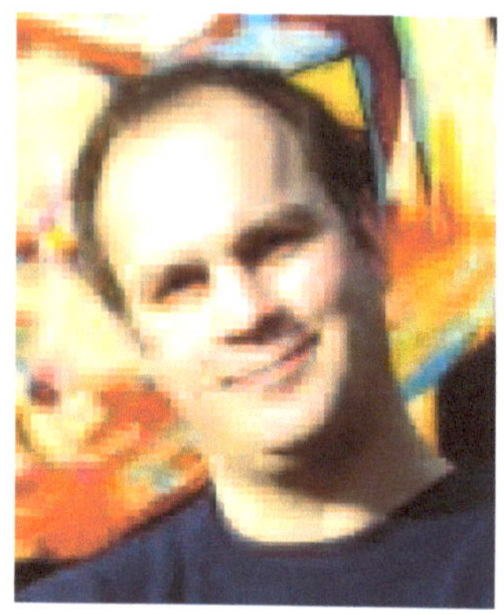

Paul Crawford has been actively involved in the visual arts community since 1990, and over the past 23 years he has owned a public gallery, been a private art consultant, worked as the Director/Curator of the Grand Forks Art Gallery (2002 – 2006) and the Penticton Art Gallery (2006 – present). Over this time he has sat on numerous boards and is currently on the boards of Island Mountain Arts in Wells, BC and the Okanagan School of the Arts in Penticton.

He is the co-founder and producer of the annual International One Minute Play Festival, is a co-producer of the annual ArtsWells Festival of All Things Art and is the associated publisher of BC Musician Magazine. He is frequently invited as a lecturer, writer, and juror and is an outspoken advocate for the arts. He is a member of the Canadian Museums Association, the British Columbia Museums Association and the Canadian Art Museums Directors Association.

He worked as an advisor to the Joe Plaskett Foundation, establishing their current relationship and partnership with the Royal Canadian Academy of the Arts, awarding a recent Canadian fine arts graduate with an annual $25,000 prize to travel internationally. He is a noted scholar on Canadian art and has amassed a unique collection of Canadian and international art.

In 2012, Paul was nominated by the Penticton Chamber of Commerce as Business Leader of the year.

Julia Trops

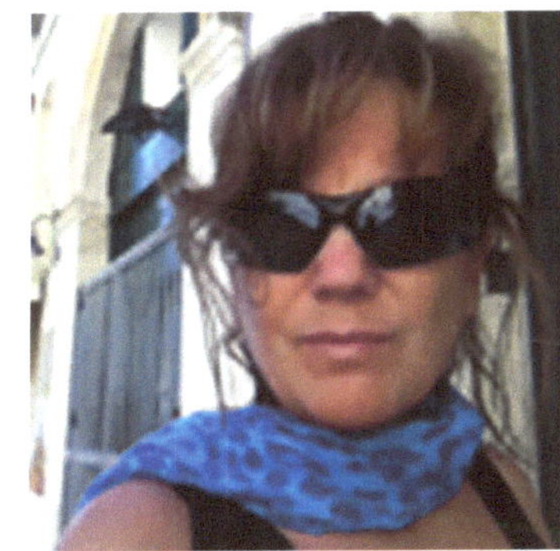

Upon moving to Kelowna 2002, she has taught, trained life drawing models, and was the sole founding organizer of the weekly Life Drawing sessions at the RCA. These sessions began the development of the non profit life drawing group, incorporated two years later, known as Livessence Society of Figurative Artists and Models.

Trops continues to be a leader in the presentation of the annual Okanagan Erotic Art Show, which she founded with two other artists in 2007 who have since followed other paths. Heavily involved in the arts community, a museum board director, a founder of Livessence, co-founder of Okanagan Arts Awards (as part of the Arts Council of the Central Okanagan), and the Okanagan Erotic Art Show, Julia keeps pretty busy in her studio, having sold over 1000 works worldwide since 2004.

With a love of books and working on encouraging other artists to get their name in print, since 2009, Julia compiled the Okanagan Erotic Art Show Catalog and the 2010 Simplicity in Mind for Livessence.

In 2011, Julia was shortlisted for the City of Kelowna's Honour in the Arts. Julia shows at Gallery Odin at Silver Star Mountain.

www.JuliaTrops.com
www.VenusIsRising.com

Sharon Lancaster

Submissions Assistant

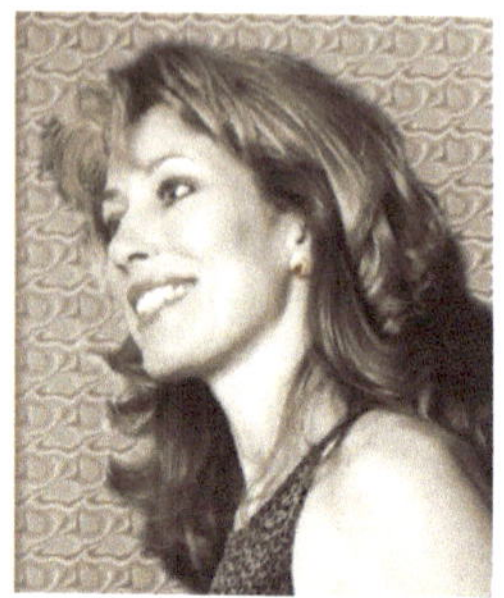

Eroticism may be defined as a state of sexual arousal or anticipation of such, dependent not just upon the individual's sexual morality, but the culture and time that the individual resides in as well.

Derived from the name of the Greek God Eros (aka Cupid) it soon became the word for romantic or sexual love. We use forms of Erotica to stimulate our senses and evoke feelings of sexual arousal and an awareness of our physical body through erotic images, sounds, touches, tastes and smells.

But these are all just words, cluttering up the page, used like Phantom Masks to hide the fantasy's and thoughts hidden in the darkest recesses of our minds, waiting for an artist, a writer, a dancer or musician to stretch our imagination, push our limitations and invite us to turn the page to ....Secrets Unspoken.

The Artists

Aarron Laidig
Alexandra Edmonds
Annemarie Fux
April Bosshard
Brenda Maunders
Calvin Bradbury
Carrie Harper
Catherine Dalfort
Christine Allan
Cynthia Gibson
Dan McCormack
Daniel McKellar
Debby Merkel
Deborah Rehm
Dirk Hiel
Edward Vincent
Elizabeth Kozlowski
Foster Gauley
Gary Mitchell
Gracie Ackerman
Greg Riley
Jacqueline Grosser
Jaine Buse
James Postill
Jan Dawson
Jan Little
Jennifer Burrows
Jessika LaFramboise
Johann Wessels
Julia Trops
Julie-Ann Miller
June Seed
Keith Funk
Kena Cumming Cormier
Kendi Clearwater
Kim Walker
Kim-Alan Dawson
Krista Berrigan
Kristine Lee
Laurel Fredin
Lawrence Cormier
Linda Franklin
Lisa Figueroa
Lynn Erin
Margot
Mario Vucinovec
Marissa Brown & Avery De Rousie
Michelle Stephenson
Nicholas Vincent
Nina Kuriloff
Pat DeLuca
Peggy Stel
Robert Canaga
Robert Simkins
Robyn Gold
Ron West
Rory O'Neill
Roxi Sim Hermsen
Ryan Robson
Sarah Parsons
Shannon Holand
Sharon Lancaster
Sharon Rose
Shaz
Suzanne LeStage
Tina Siddiqui
Trina Ganson
Una Connor, Chad Henderson
Victoria Pendragon
Victoria Skofteby

Aarron Laidig

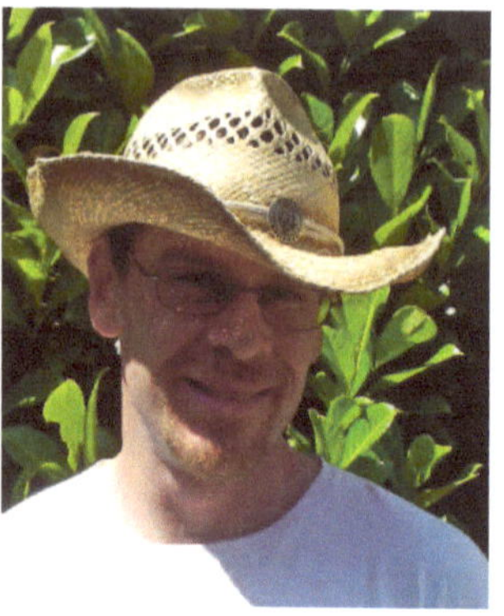

Aarron Laidig is a self described libertine, coffee addict, and lifelong artist. When not pursuing his favorite pastimes of seeking out new sexual shenanigans to partake in, savoring a good latte, or making visual eye candy he can usually be found enjoying a good book.

www.Aarron.com

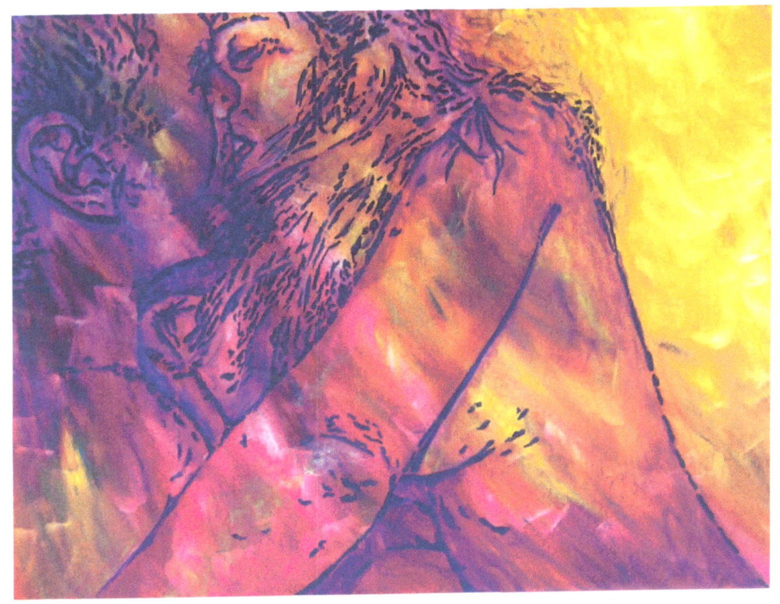

Memory of a Dream
Aarron Laidig
12x16
Acrylic on canvas

Time...
It changes things, but the moments exist forever.

Alexandra Edmonds

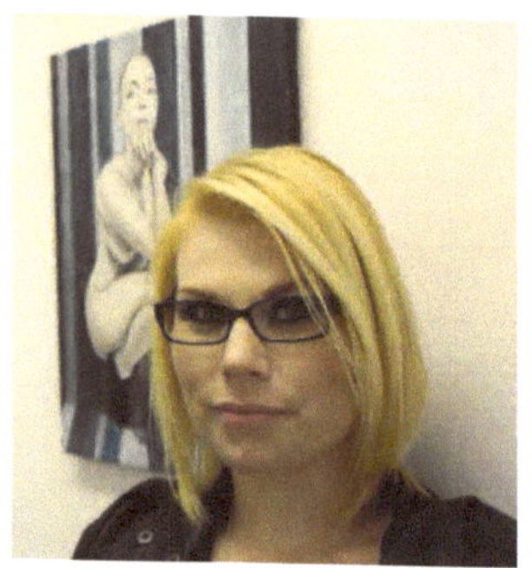

Alexandra Edmonds is a Canadian artist working in painting, most notably in portraits. Her work explores the psychology of relationships, beauty and women's identity in a post feminist era. Her portraits question the distance between subject and viewer and how we look at people. Alexandra grew up in the picturesque Okanagan Valley in BC, Canada. She studied painting at l'École National Supérieure des Beaux-Arts in Paris, France, at the University of British Columbia Okanagan in Canada and Central Saint Martins College of Art and Design in London, UK. She received her BFA in 2009 and her MA in Fine Art at Central Saint Martins in 2011.

www.AlexEdmondsArt.ca

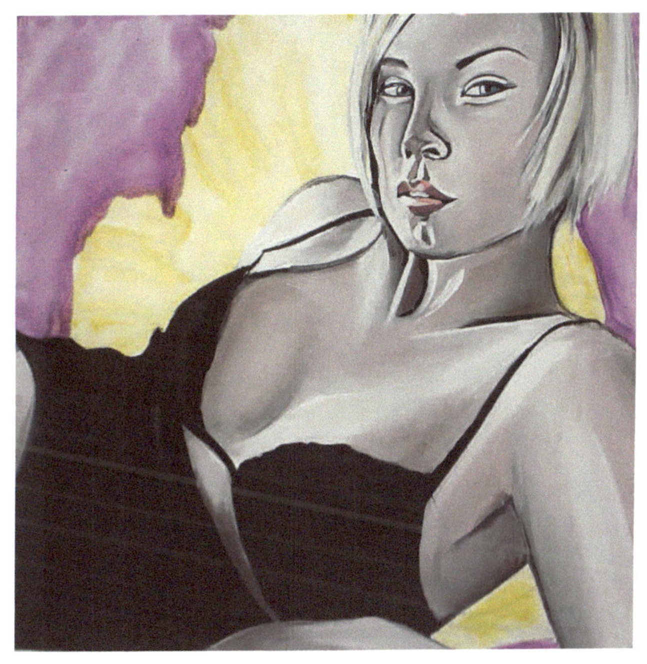

From Paris With Love
Alexandra Edmonds
16x16
Oil on canvas

Keeping the romance alive from abroad

Annemarie Fux

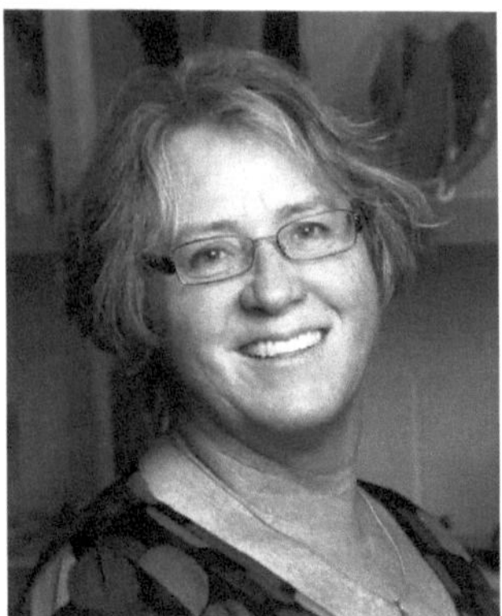

My name is Annmarie Fux and I grew up in the midst of the Swiss Alps where I taught in a small school with a spectacular view. In 1980, I came to Canada and my view became the Rocky Mountains. Since 1988, I have come to love the gentle hills that frame the lakes of the Okanagan.

In 2002, I graduated with a Bachelor of Fine Arts from Okanagan University College, now University of British Columbia Okanagan. Sculpting, painting, drawing and photography are an intrinsic part of me, but when I had the chance to work and learn in a glass fusing studio, that became my passion. In January 2011, I set up my own Art Glass Studio in West Kelowna.

www.aFuxArtGlass.com

Photo credit: Christian Reiner

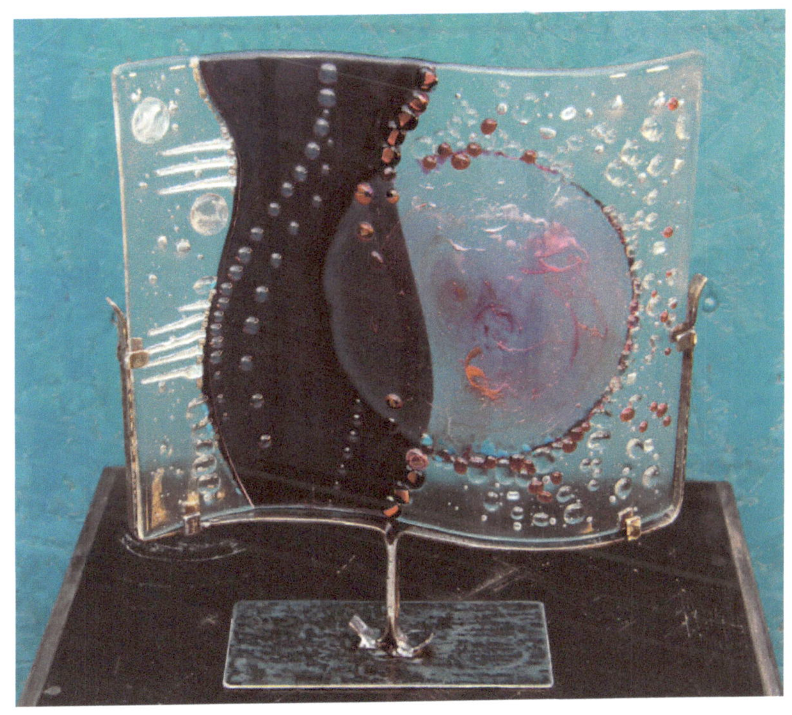

Sleeping Bud
Annemarie Fux
5 1/2 x13 1/4
Fused glass on metal stand

A first awakening of the senses.

April Bosshard

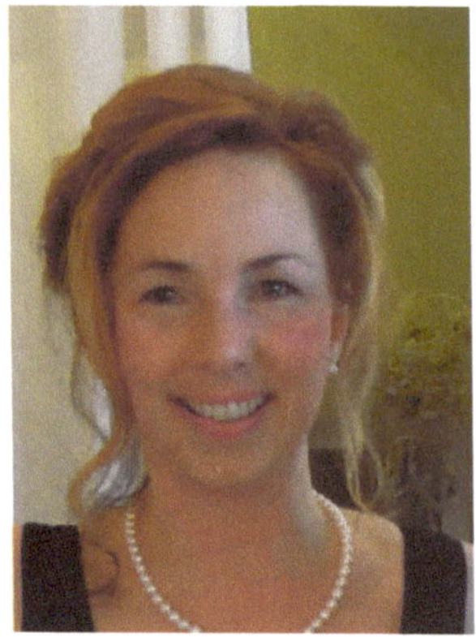

I am a self-taught painter who has studied independently with a handful of contemporary artists. My past experience in film production and creative writing laid a strong foundation to explore and expand my creativity on canvas. I am a sensualist at heart, and I love using the sensual medium of oils to create images that capture the sensuality of human experience and perception. Being a writer as well as a painter, I often like to incorporate words into my images. I live and work on Bowen Island in Southern British Columbia.

www.AprilBosshard.com

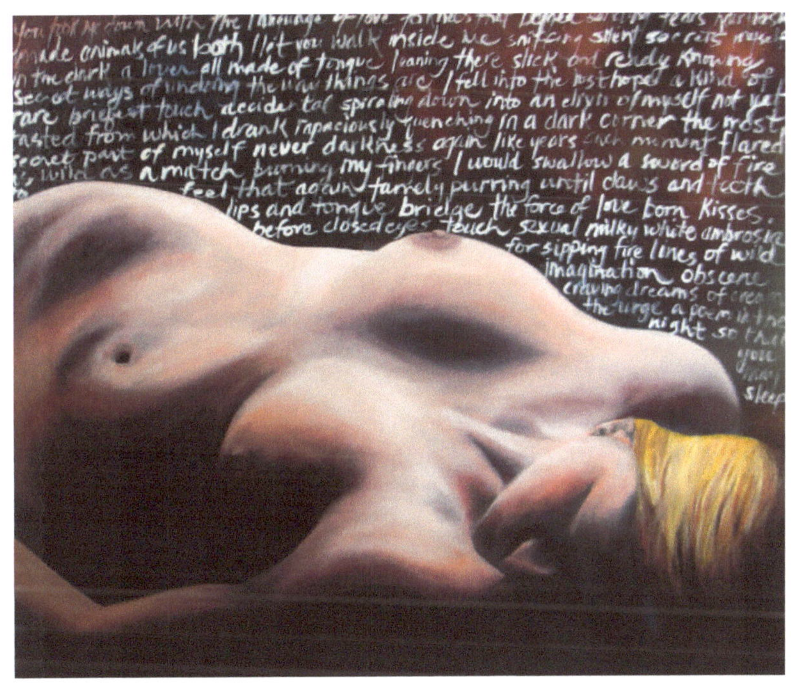

Take Me Back
Arpril Bosshard
20x24
Oil on Canvas

Words, in the form of thoughts, memories or speech, invisibly surround our bodies all the time, and more often than not, they contain erotic undertones.

Brenda Maunders

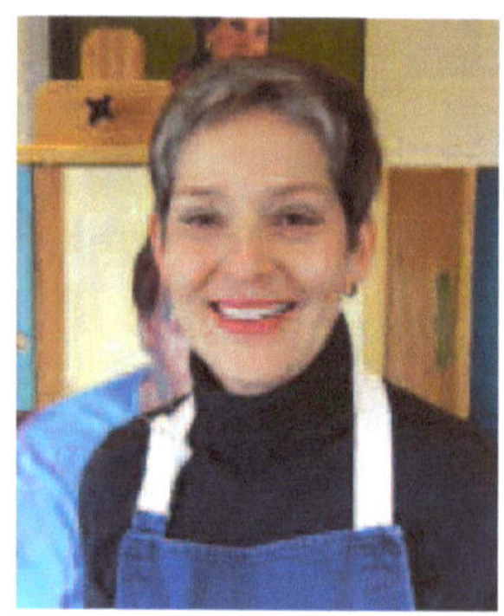

Stories. It's all about stories. Everyone has a story — happy, sad, humdrum, mysterious. Some are private, some public. Some tug at your heartstrings; others grab you by the throat. Still others make you ponder the past, imagine the future, or long for the road not taken. Our lives are nothing more than stories we write ourselves. If you're not happy with yours, change it. I did.

www.BrendaMaunders.com

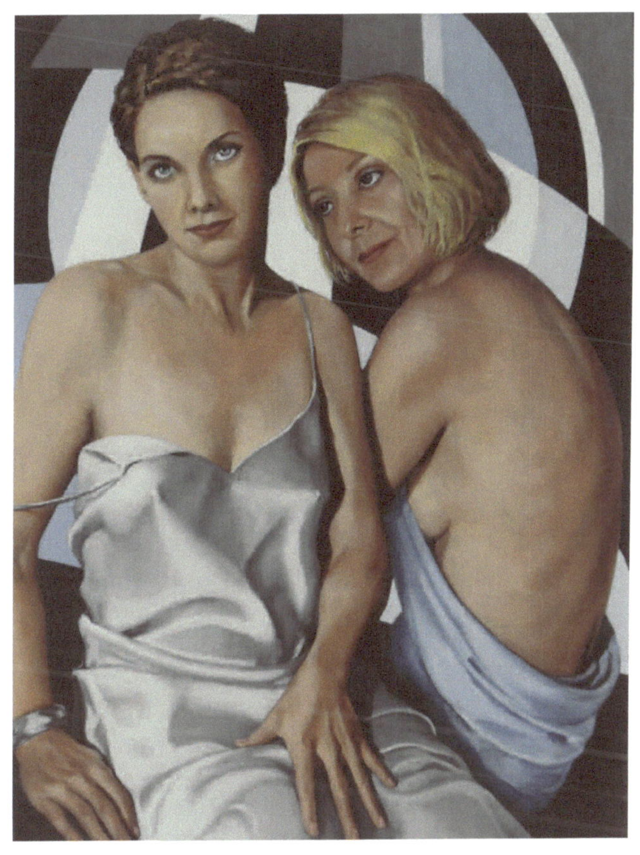

Saturday night… and Sunday morning
Brenda Maunders
15x19
Oil on canvas

Unlike you, I don't care who knows.

Calvin Bradbury

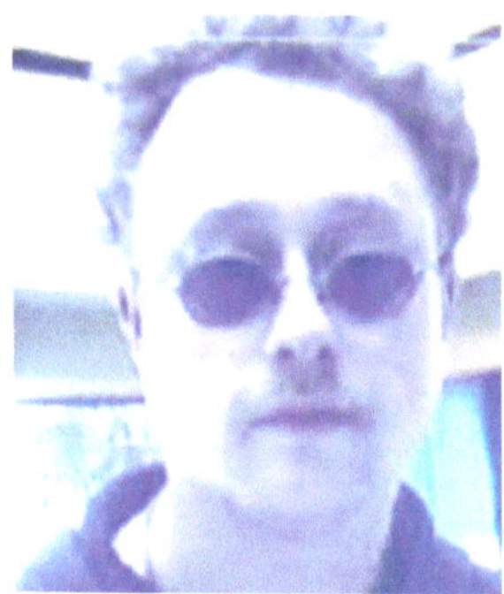

Calvin is a self-taught Artist originally from Nova Scotia who has lived in West Coast Canada for many years. While we can accept that the technical development of his paintings as progressive, to believe that Bradbury has not professionally studied is a phenomena. Spending time on the margins of society in some periods of his life, art has carried Bradbury through the vicissitudes of the peripheral. The attitude toward his work is to avoid mainstream style and ideas and realize his own vision.

www.myartclub.com/artist.php?xyz=1217

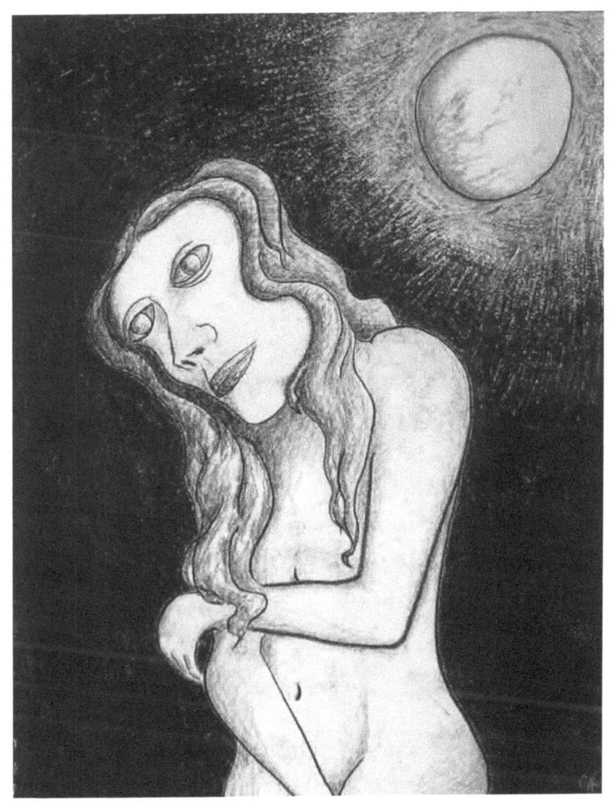

Drawing down the Moon
Calvin Bradbury
14x18
Charcoal and chalk on paper

The heavens were jealous, as she waited in and as the stars came out to gaze on the creature, so relinquished by the night.

Carrie Harper

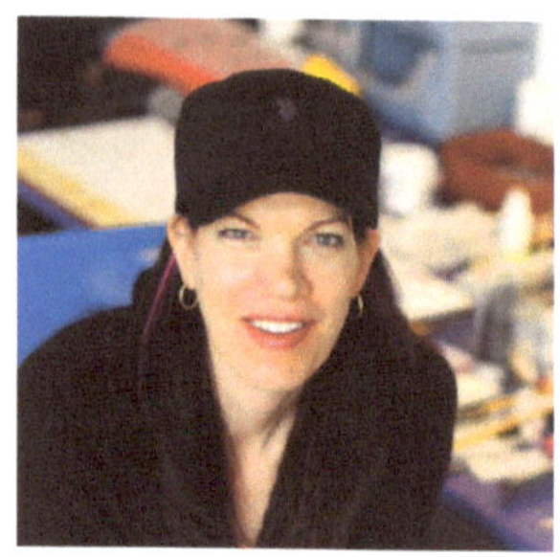

I experiment, change things and push boundaries in my whole life, not just my art. Mixed Media, not just another way to make art but a culture of limitless creative experience, what my hungry soul yearns for! I've learned to draw faces and figures using my interpretation of the Golden Ratio; Davinci's methods made easy. Wading deep into a meditative artistic experience using collage as a base and experimenting with such airbrush paint and ink, acrylic mediums, paper, block prints, photography, epoxy resin, beeswax etc.........

www.thepearworkshop.com
www.heARTschoolkelowna.com

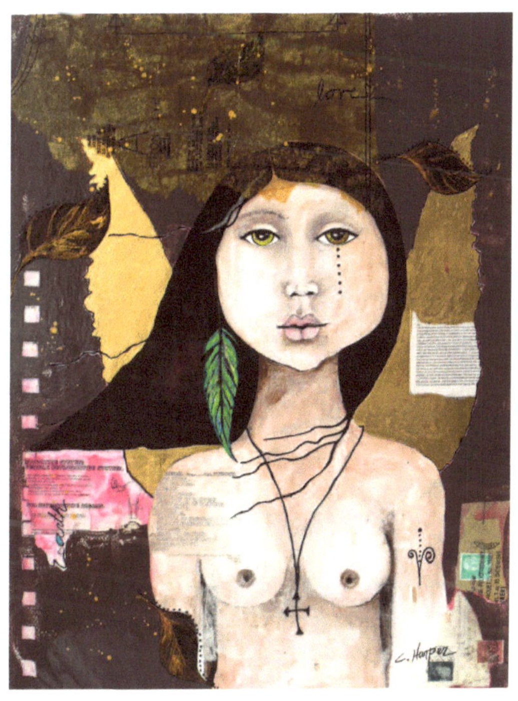

Naked Girl I, Terra
Carrie Harper
18x24
Mixed Media on panel

Naked Girl 1 is an Earth fertility archetype created intuitively.

Catherine Dalfort

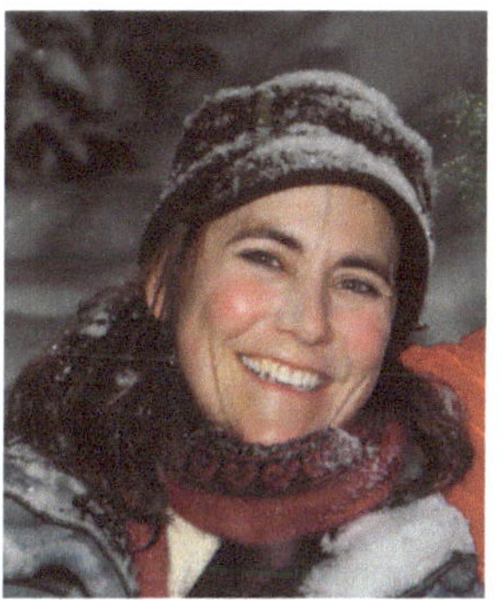

I studied printmaking and photography at the University of Calgary and have since moved to Barriere, BC. I live on a small farm on the North Thompson River with my partner Alan and our 5 year old daughter Isabella. I have a print studio in my home and I enjoy working on the human form in its natural and adorned state. I definitely have a fascination for the secrets of the psyche that lie in the imagery of tattoos and adornments of the flesh.

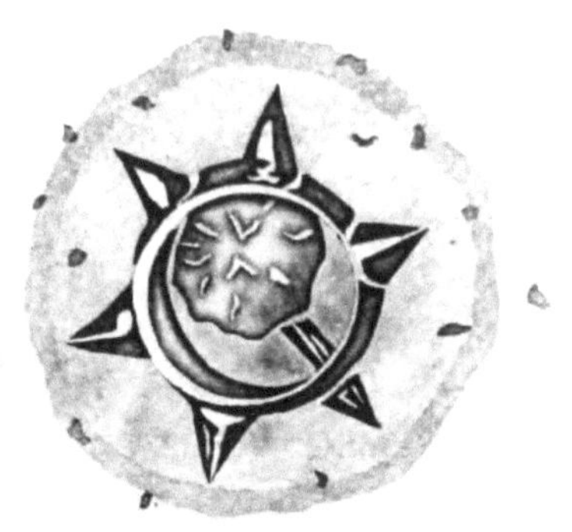

Piercing
Catherine Dalfort
11x14
Copper etching

Pain me, Pleasure me

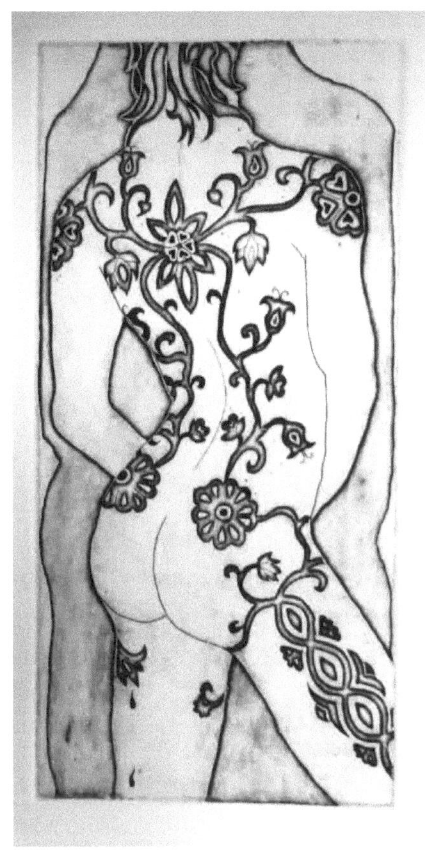

Red River Girl
Catherine Dalfort
16x24
Copper etching

Wouldn't you like to see my blossoms?

Christine Allan

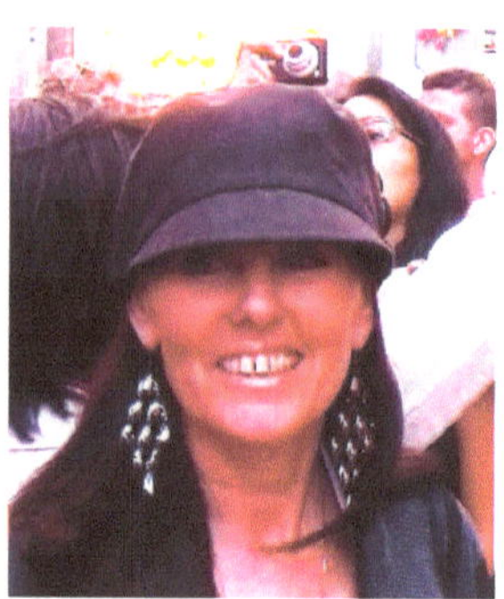

Christine Allan, lives in Chemainus, BC, with her husband and two daughters. She is a mostly self-taught artist who has been creating art in one way or another for most of her life. Art is a passion as well as a refuge for her. Painting is how she deals with the turmoil that is sometimes part of our world. Christine has overcome many obstacles in her life and strongly believes in the healing power of art. She does commissions and regularly donates pieces to raise funds for Cancer research and supports The Art for Healing Foundation.

www.ChrisAllanDesigns.com

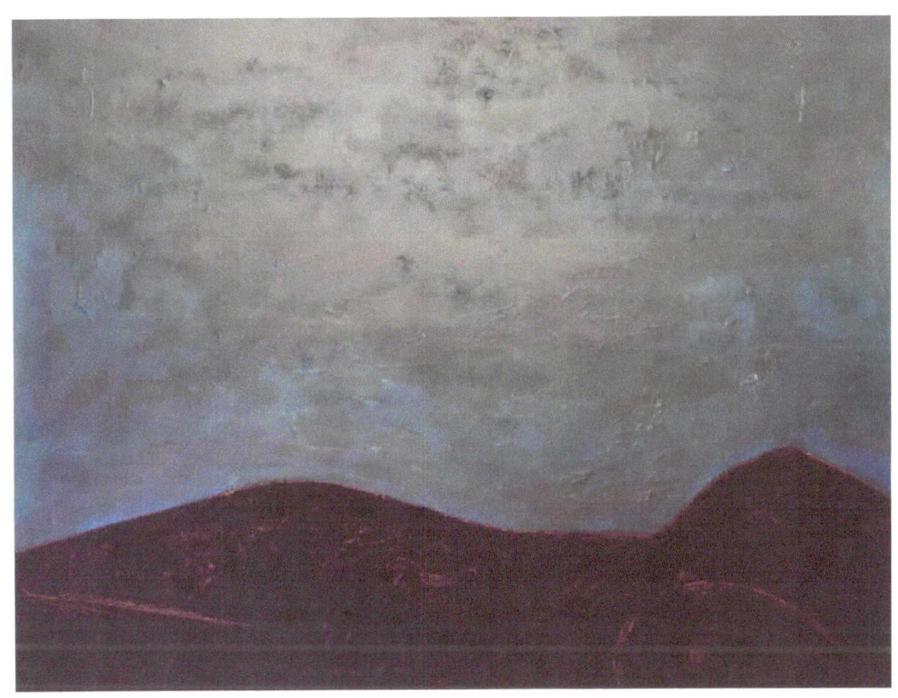

My Starry Night
Christine Allan
30x24'
Mixed Media

Sometimes the body becomes part of the landscape

Cynthia Gibson

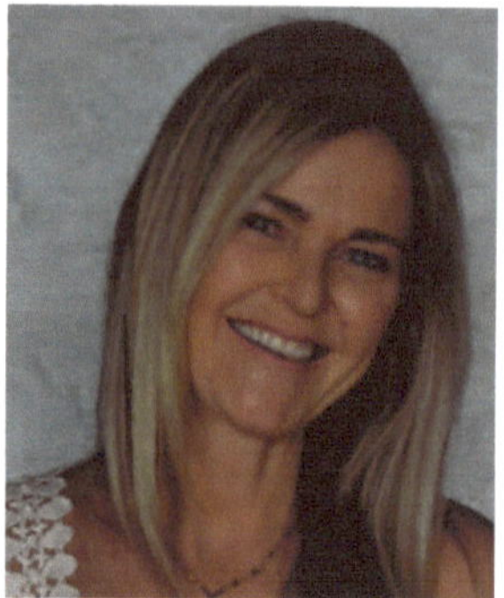

Cynthia lives and works in West Kelowna BC. She is passionate about motorcycle riding that she took up at 50 mainly because it frightened her and now she can't imagine not riding! Why did she wait so long? Her heart belongs to the great outdoors. She loves to garden, fish, and hike through the bush. Her dream is to build a little white house with a wraparound porch where she can dream on a hammock. Close friends and family are the most cherished things in her life.

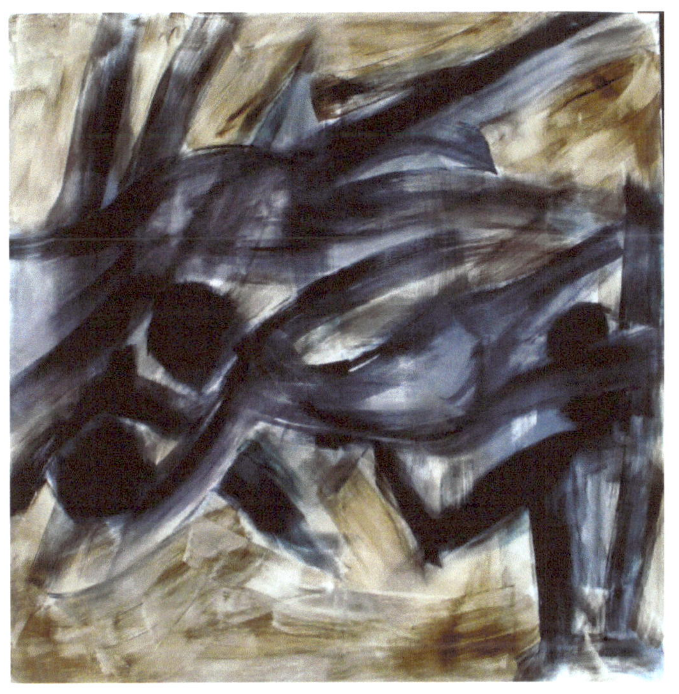

Sexual Abandon
Cynthia Gibson
39.25x39.25
Acrylic

My "swinger friend" inspired this free-stroke painting as she tried to describe to me the feeling of making love to numerous people at a time.

Dan McCormack

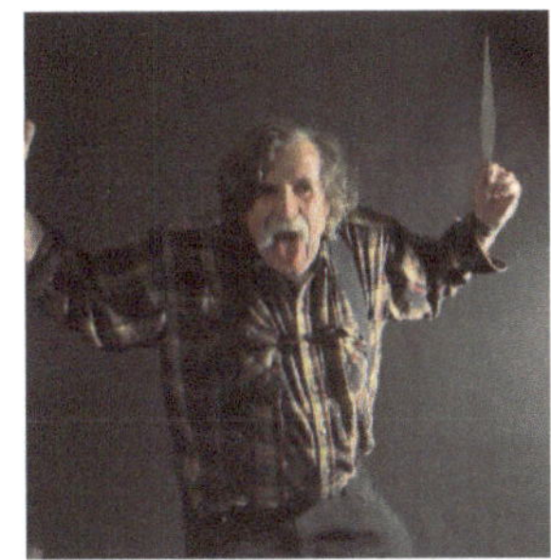

I earned an MFA in Photography from the School of the Art Institute of Chicago over forty years ago and I have been creating personal photographic imagery consistently since. I first began photographing the nude with Wendy, whom I married in 1968 and I am still married to. I have worked exclusively with the nude as a theme but I have explored varied processes, techniques and cameras. I won a NYSCA CAPS Fellowship in Photography in 1982 and the Ultimate Eye Foundation Fellowship for Figurative Photography in 2009. I currently head the Photography area at Marist College in Poughkeepsie, NY.

www.DanMcCormack.net

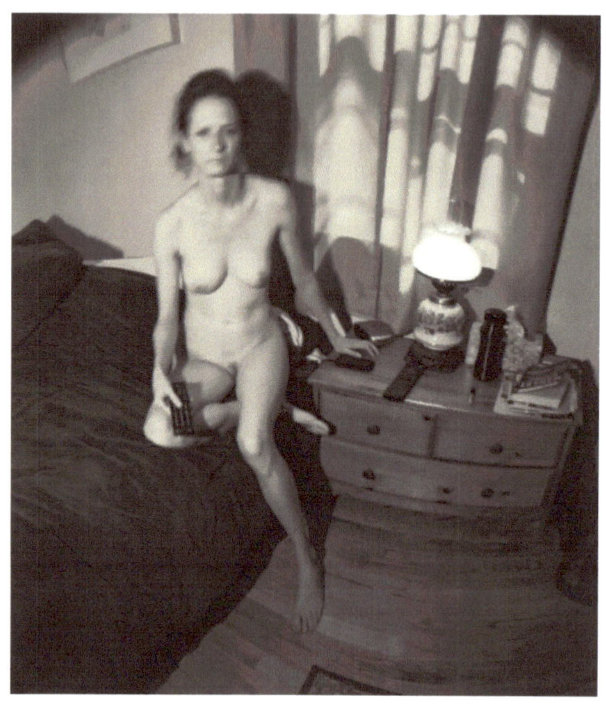

Bridget_L_5-20-12--11AB
Dan McCormack
20x16
Pinhole Camera digital pigment print

Pinhole camera portrait of Bridget nude at home in Rhinebeck NY.

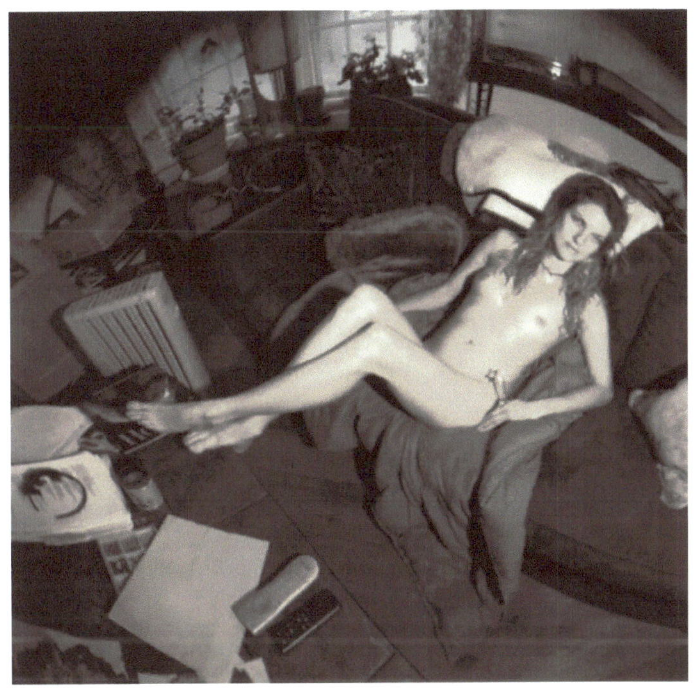

Helen_W_12-12-12--09AC
Dan McCormack
20x16
Pinhole Camera digital pigment print

Pinhole camera image of Helen nude at home in High Falls NY

Daniel McKellar

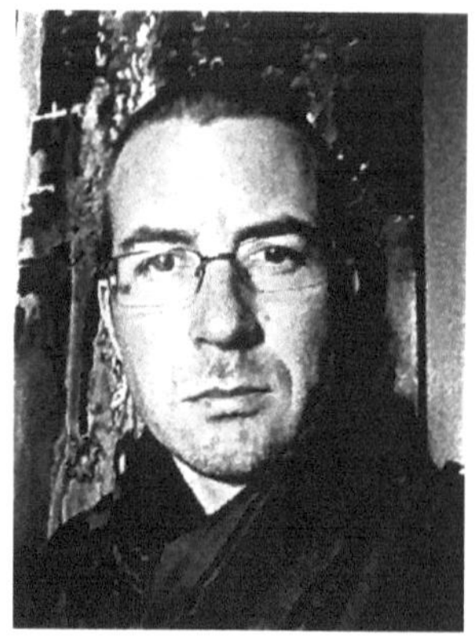

Originally from the Northern Interior of British Columbia, I have been drawing since the age of three. Being self taught, I began to experiment with technique at an early age studying the works of Michaelangelo, Frank Frazetta and Dali in books. I was also influenced by various relatives that are painters, sculptors and musicians. Moving to Vancouver in my early twenties, I discovered and pursued another favorite art form, acting. Like an irresistible urge however I needed to keep painting, and began showing pieces in various group exhibitions, coffee shops and nightclubs. Now residing in Kelowna, BC, my perceptions of the human condition and my willingness to surrender to intuitive impulse continue to add passion and creativity in my work.

www.DanielMcKellar.com

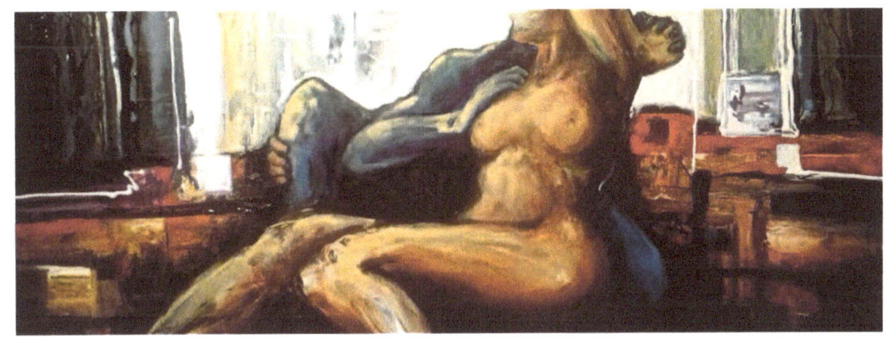

Windows
Daniel McKellar
80x30
Oil/mixed on board

Like stained glass, we see through to the light.

Debby Merkel

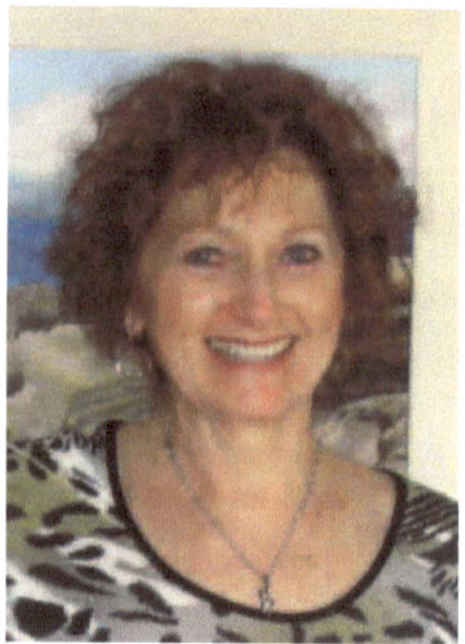

Debby was born on Vancouver Island at Ladysmith, BC. She was raised in Alberta and returned to the province of her birth in 1972. Debby relocated to Kelowna in 2012 after living in Penticton for over two decades. She is drawn to the arts in any form and is a blues lover. When not painting, she enjoys walking, hiking, biking, hooking up with friends for coffee, the latest flick at the theatre, or reading.

www.DebbyMerkel.com

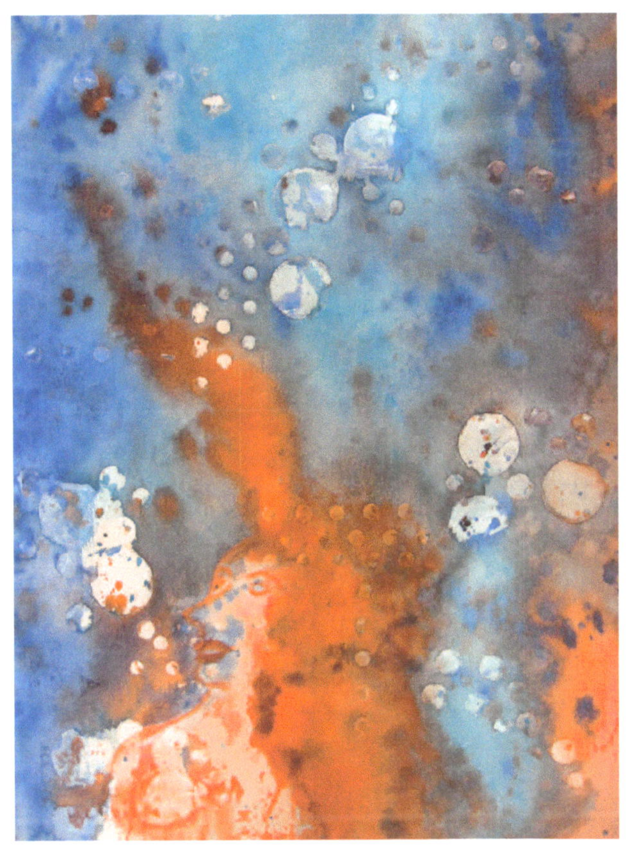

Bliss
Debby Merkel
15-3/4x12-3/4
Watercolour/Mixed Media

Like that first burst of chocolate that explodes in your mouth... taste it?

Deborah Rehm

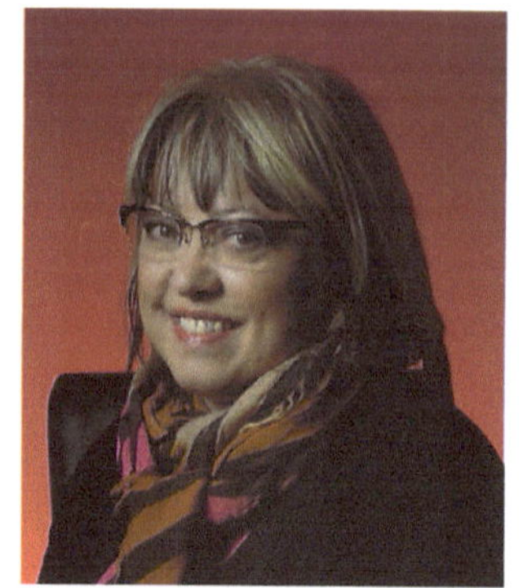

Deborah Rehm is a local emerging artist. Although she has a full time career in management, she has pursued photography and digital arts with unbridled passion since 2010. She loves the endless possibilities these two mediums offer in exploring the beauty and sensuality all around us. She has earned several awards and honorable mentions for her images evaluated by her local photography club. This year she also had two images selected by the photo club to compete in CAPA competitions.

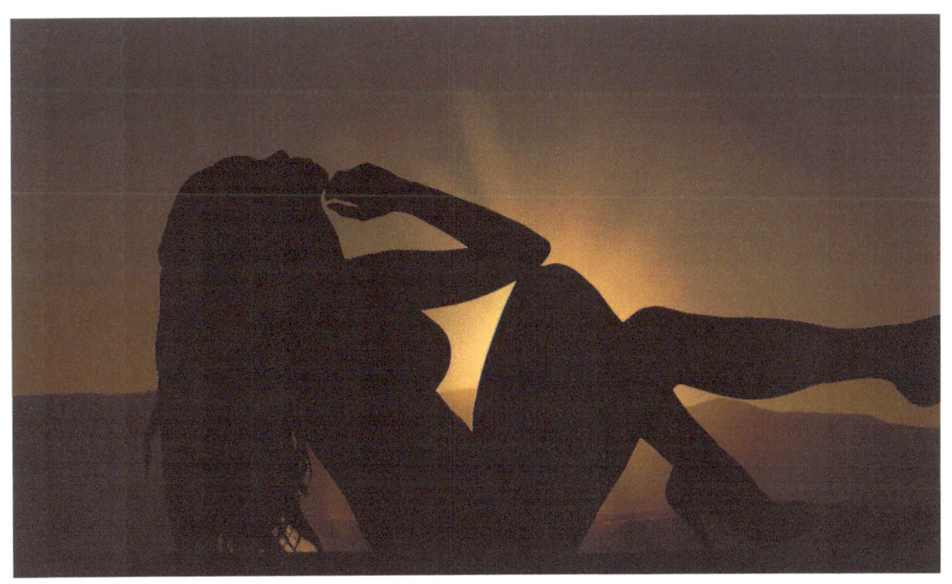

Dreaming
Deborah Rehm
16x20
Photography

Dreaming for the moment when eager hands and half-formed thoughts collide.

Dirk Hiel

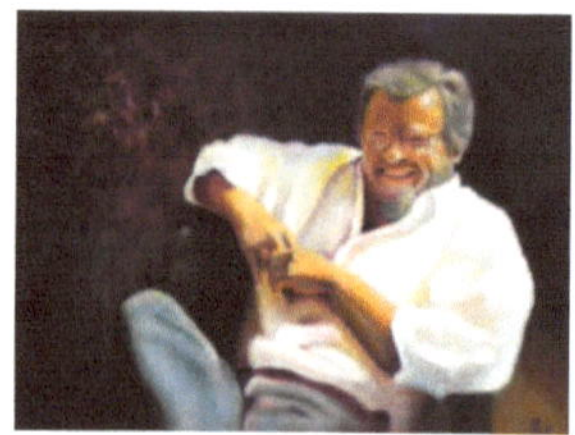

Dirk Hiel is a Dutch-born portrait painter. He divides his time between Edmonton, Alberta, and Kelowna, British Columbia, Canada. Dirk likes to do 20-30 commissioned portraits per year in an old-master style with a touch of impressionism. Dirk's work can be found in more than 99 private collections.

http://www.saatchionline.com/profile/92497

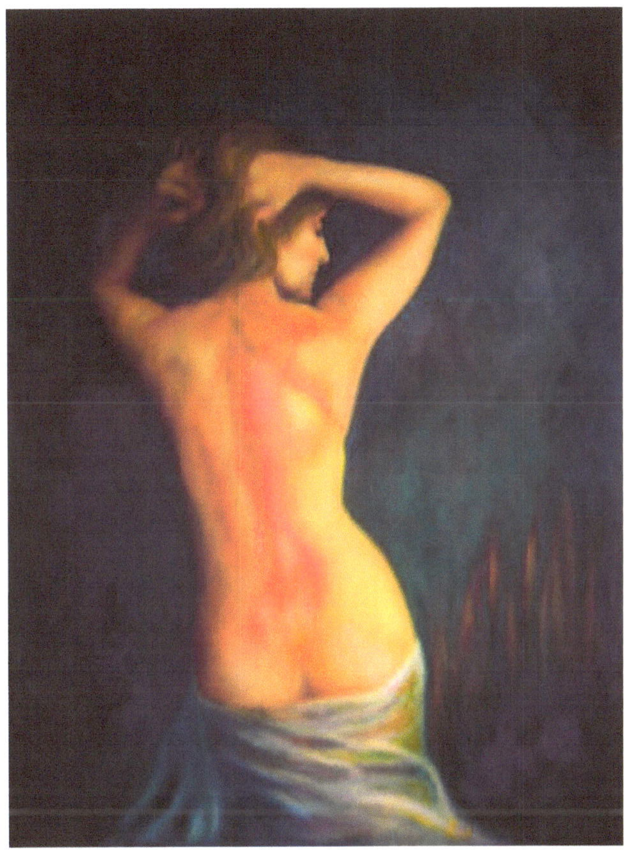

Renaissance
Dirk Hiel
35x45
Oil on canvas

This beautiful woman is about to reveal her secret self.

Edward Vincent

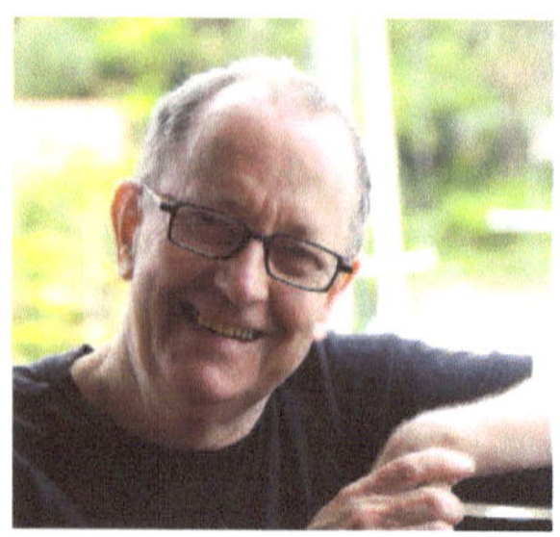

I have been an illustrator for over thirty years, mixing this where possible with fine art. Over the years I have completed thousands of 'artist's impressions', as well as portraits in watercolour and oil and commissioned boardroom pieces. Painting the human form remains my main focus, as nothing quite matches the feeling, emotion and energy; essential ingredients to any fine work. I'm presently developing a body of work focusing on figures and landscapes, to be available this Spring.

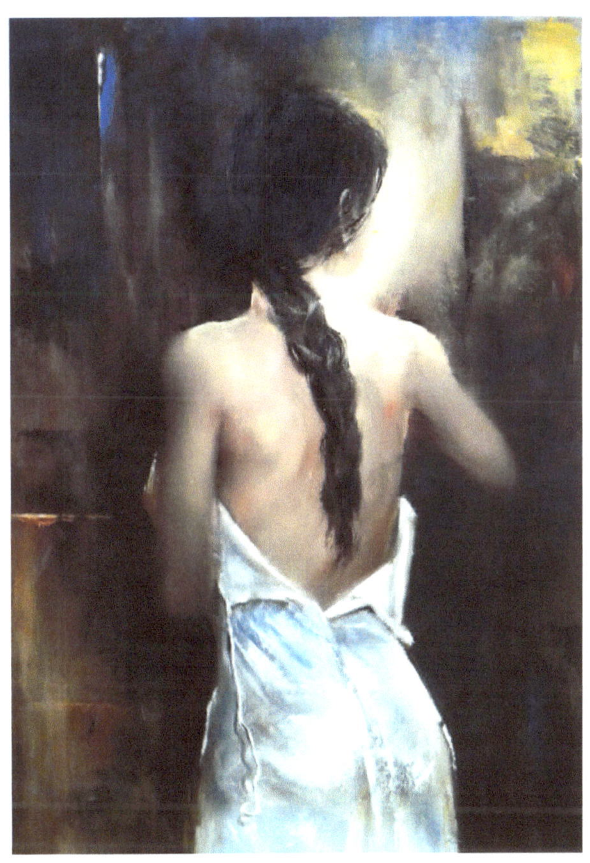

Invitation
Edward Vincent
31x21
Oil on Gessoed Art Paper, bonded to board

Help me with this would you darling?

Elizabeth Kozlowski

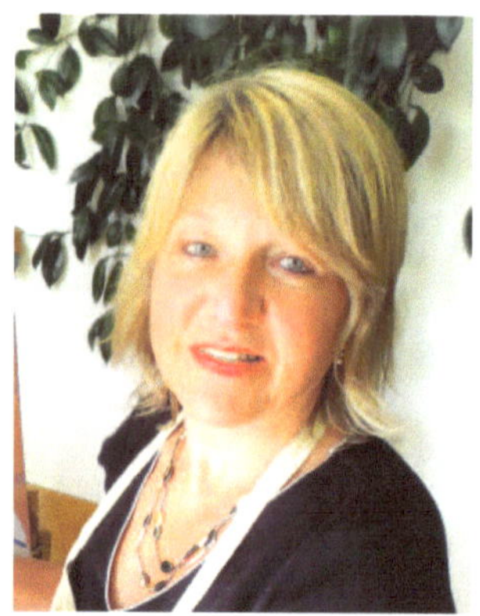

Elizabeth K. grew up in Warsaw, Poland where she started her affiliation with art. As a young woman she made Canada her home and settled in North Vancouver, where she still lives and works. She is passionate about figurative expression and portraiture in oil. Elizabeth K. is a member of the Portrait Society of America and the North Vancouver Community Arts Council.

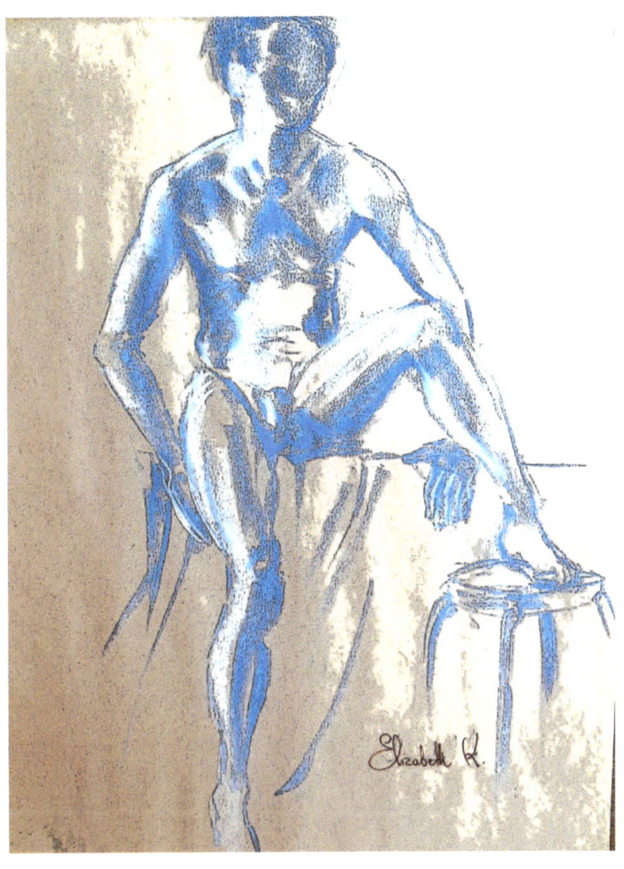

Tell me
Elizabeth Kozlowski
12x16
Drawing transferred to wood

This series of works was created based on sketches I drew in a Life Drawing Sessions.

Foster Gauley

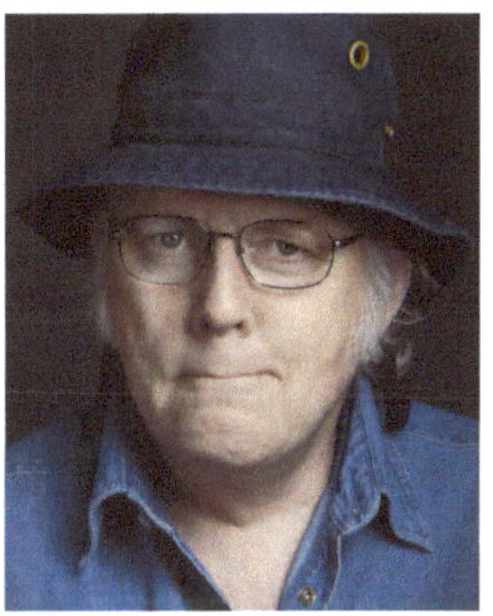

Foster is a retired firefighter, with 40 years of photography experience (and no formal training) behind him. Bored with making pretty pictures, he has decided to push the edges out a bit, making images that have many uncomfortable, and a few liking what he is doing. Have a look, see what you think.

www.FosterGauley.com

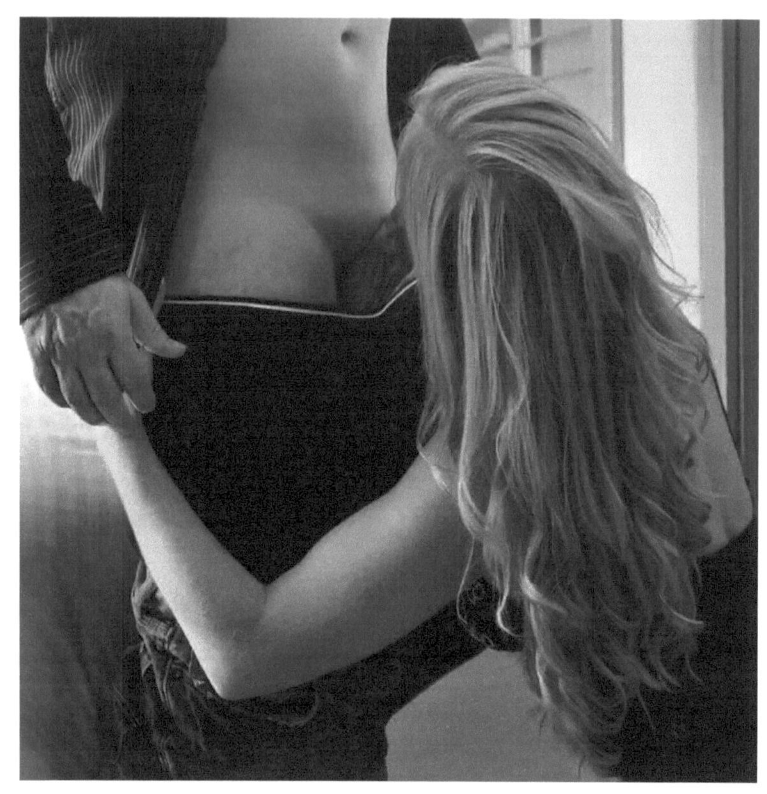

Party Favor
Foster Gauley
24x24
Photograph

-shhh, hurry, no 1 will know-

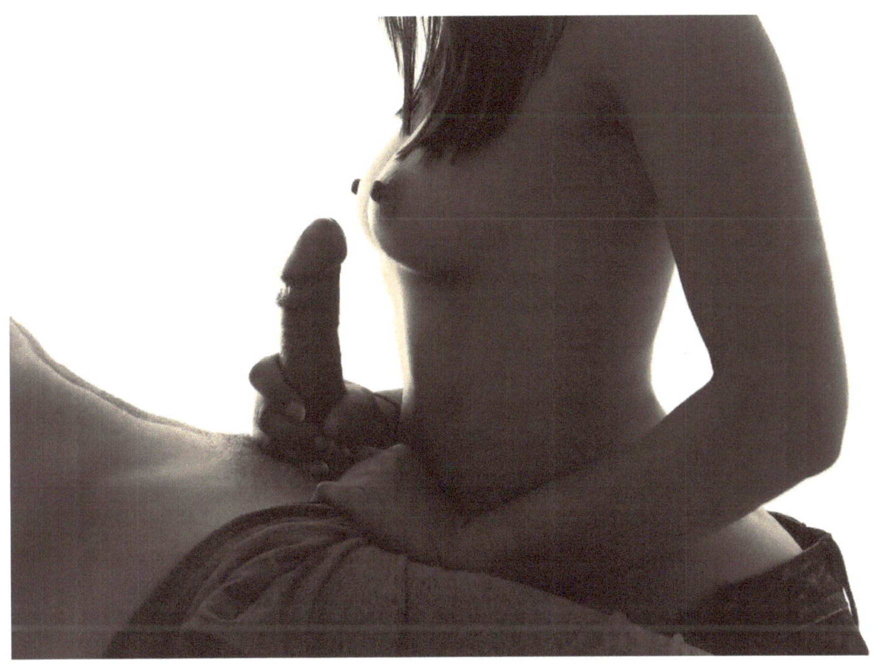

His Undivided Attention
Foster Gauley
16x24
Photograph

Now's the time to ask him, for anything!

Gary Mitchell

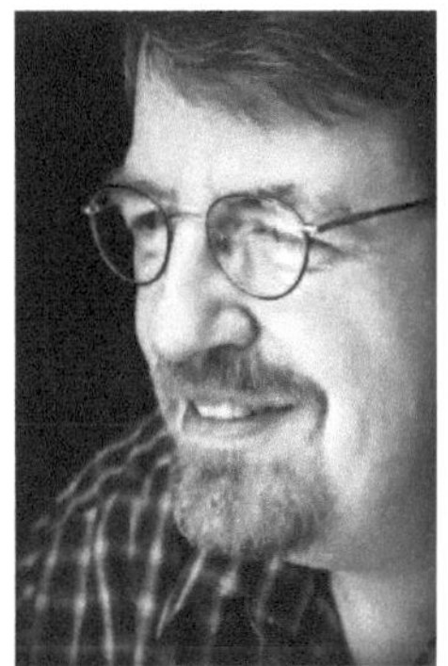

A photographer since childhood, I was taught by my father who had a darkroom in the basement. I still live in my hometown of Dayton, Ohio, where I own a small business in addition to pursuing my artwork. I also collect books, enjoy good movies and bad movies, and frequently see local bands play live in the local music venues. Have had a Canadian "pen pal" since I was in high school – Free Keith!

www.GaryM.com
www.GaryMphoto.tumblr.com
www.Facebook.com/GaryMphoto

Photo credit Michelle Waters

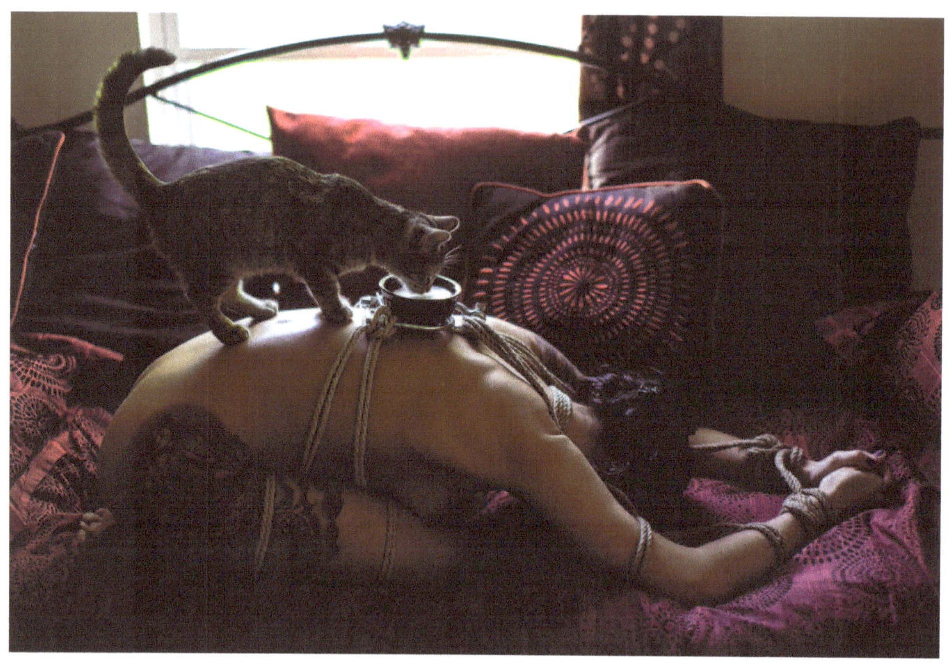

Whipped
Gary Mitchell
16x24
Photograph

A slightly exaggerated depiction of the relationship between pets and their "masters."

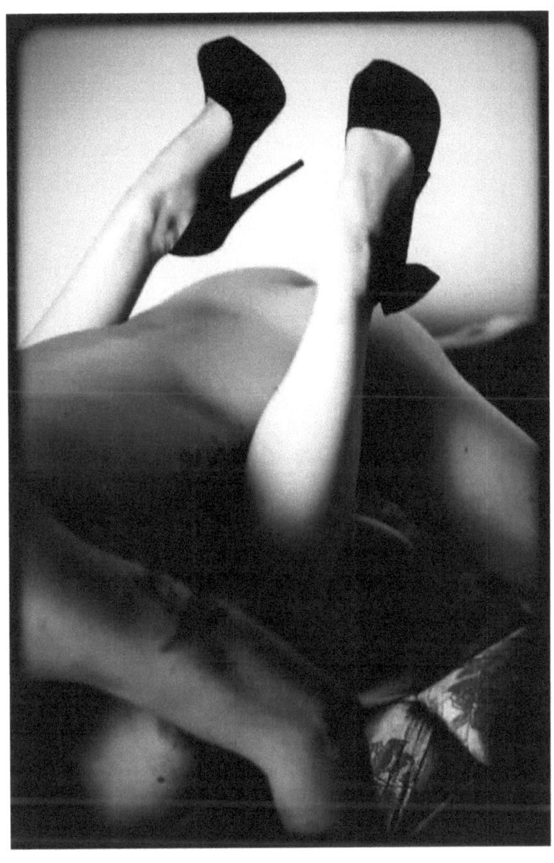

FMP
Gary Mitchell
16x24
Photograph

"Fuck Me Pumps" send a clear signal, a fetish for both men and women.

Gracie Ackerman

I am a crazy, creative single mother. I am a spiritualist and an artist that is always looking to contact the OTHER.. I live for this PASSION!

www.SexAsSacred.com

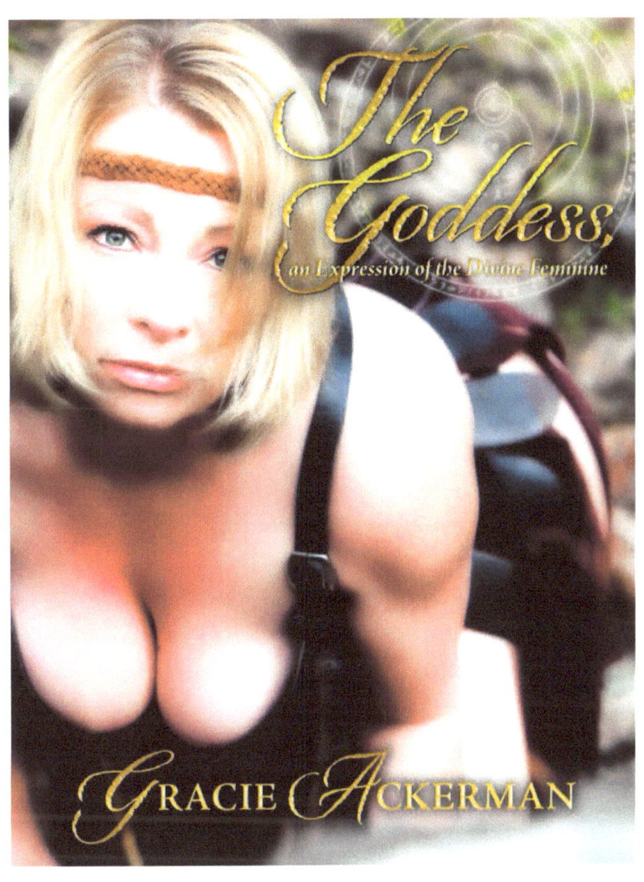

The Goddess - an Expression of the Divine Feminine\
Gracie Ackerman
Published Book 88 pages of Goddess depictions
Printed Book

Greg Riley

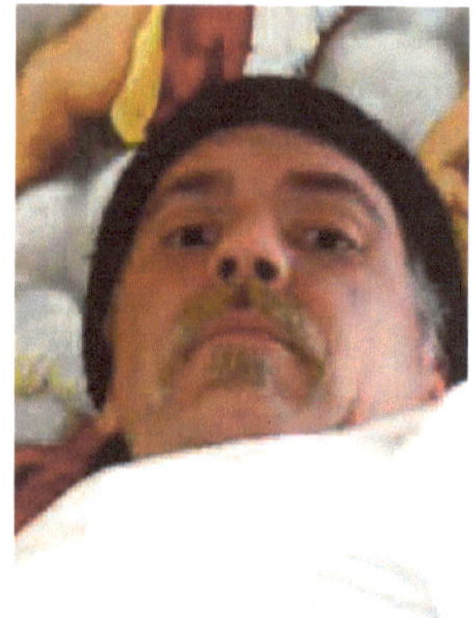

I have been an artist as long as I can remember. I am currently a mural painter by trade, but have worked as an illustrator, fine artist, sculptor, graphic artist, and portrait painter. I have been earning a living as an artist for 25 years and I am always ready to tackle the next project that comes into my studio. I studied at Joliet Junior College, American Academy of Art in Chicago, and at the Palette and Chisel Academy in Chicago. I currently live and work in the Chicago area, but have painted murals for many different areas of the country.

www.GregRileyArtWork.com

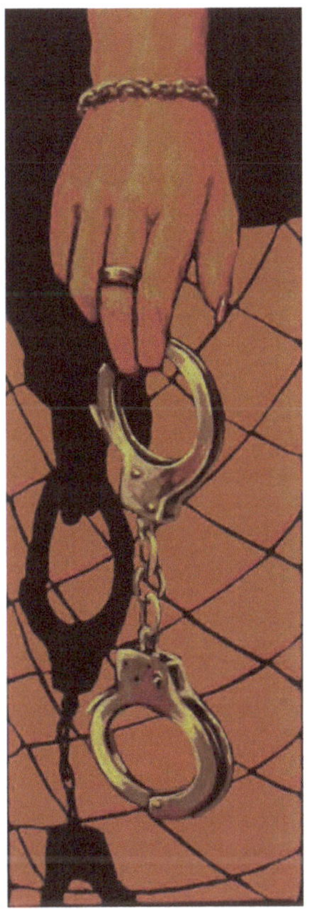

Escape Artist
Greg Riley
12x4
Acrylic

For the work Escape Artist I used the imagery to suggest escape from daily concerns, and pushing boundaries as an escape from normal routines and time worn rituals.

Jacqueline Grosser

My art is a reflection of my experiences boating, flying , roadtripping. Most of my life has been spent exploring our coastal waters, which greatly influenced my painting during this time. Two years ago I moved to the Okanagan, and as a new pilot, flying allowed me to view the hills, valleys, big skies and clouds from a different viewpoint. This aerial perspective is a new way to see for me, and art allows me the freedom to express these views in my work. The possibilities are endless.

www.JacquelineGrosser.com

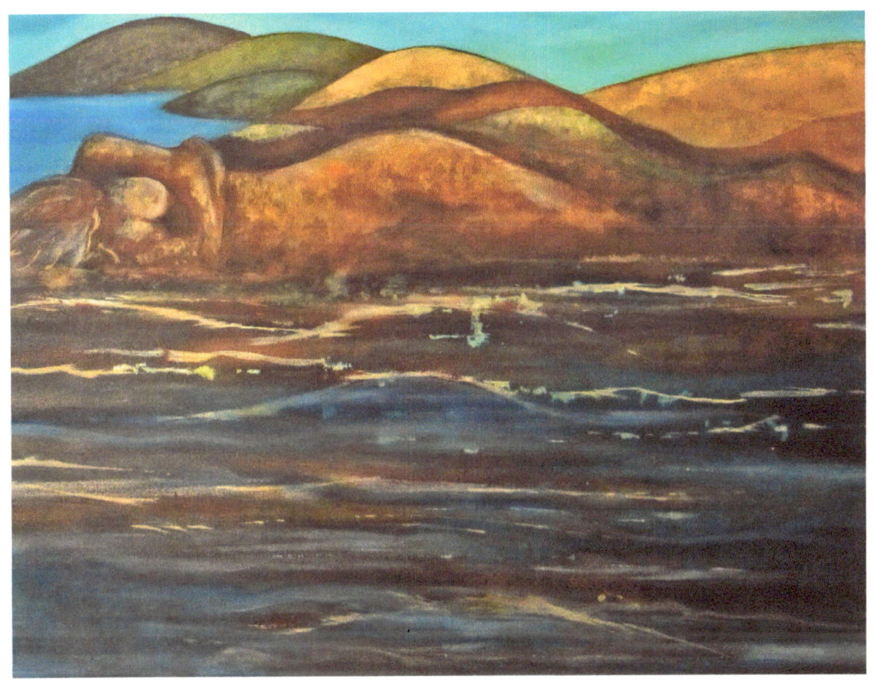

Curves
Jacqueline Grosser
36x48
Acrylic

Where Earth and Water meet...Earth for the curve of sensuality, water for the flow...

Jaine Buse

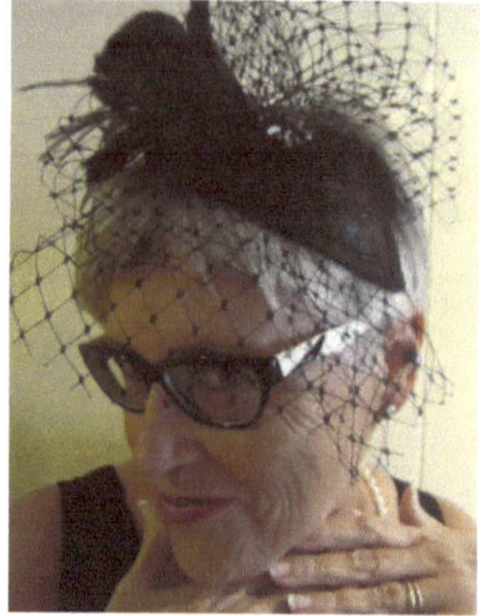

Jaine is an avid world traveler, reader, mah jong player and observer of the arts who is passionate about creating on canvas. Her love of nature, people and places is implanted into the scenes, abstract forms and figurative works that evolve through the spontaneous process. She is continually inspired from everyone in her life and loves the adrenalin rush when a "Call to Artist" goes out with a short deadline.

JainesAffordableOriginalArt.weebly.com

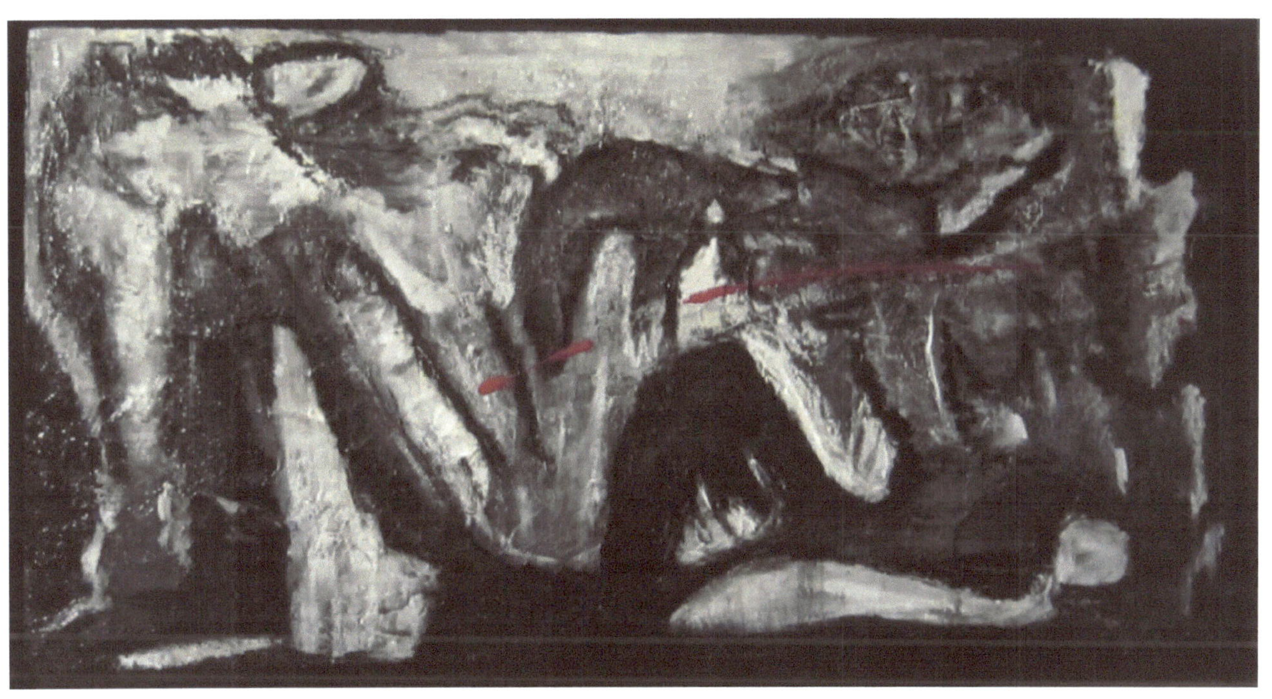

Kinky Streak
Jaine Buse
13x25x1.5
Acrylic mixed media

Seeking: Carnal Pleasures

James Postill

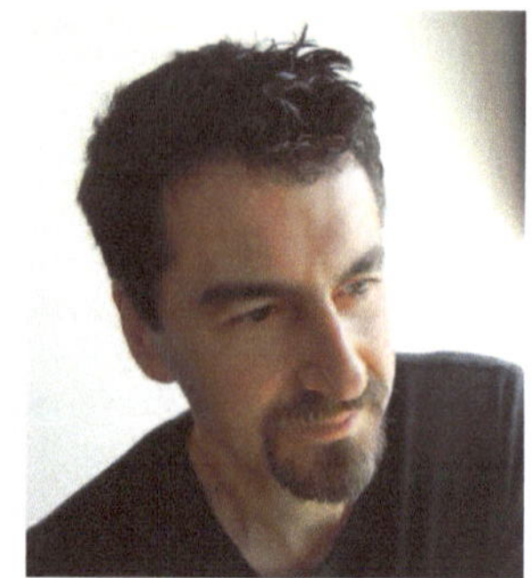

I live in Vernon, and love what I do.
I love my busy life, and am thankful
for everything that has come & gone from it, as well as
what's still due for my doorstep.

Always evolving,
I love, but try not to take too seriously,
past and future versions of myself that shift around me like desert sand.
Striving to be a perpetual student
of nature, of life, and of those who have walked the road I'm walking now.

I love my wife, my children, and the rest of my soul family.
I love where the universe has placed me.

http://www.whiterockgallery.com/James_Postill.htm

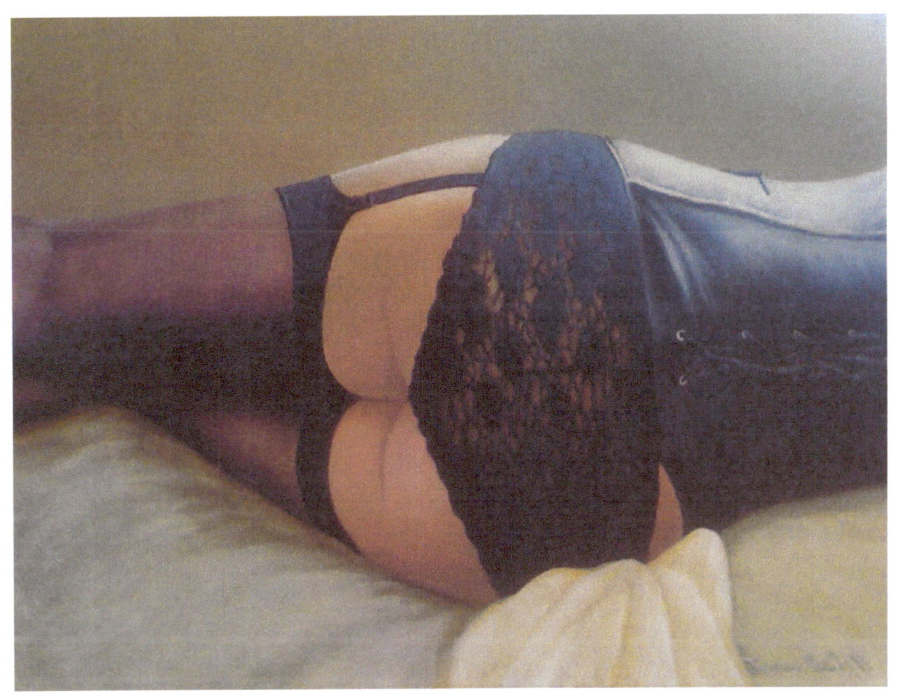

Afternoon delight
James Postill
18x24
Oil on canvas

Warm light from the window bathed her as she waited.

Jan Dawson

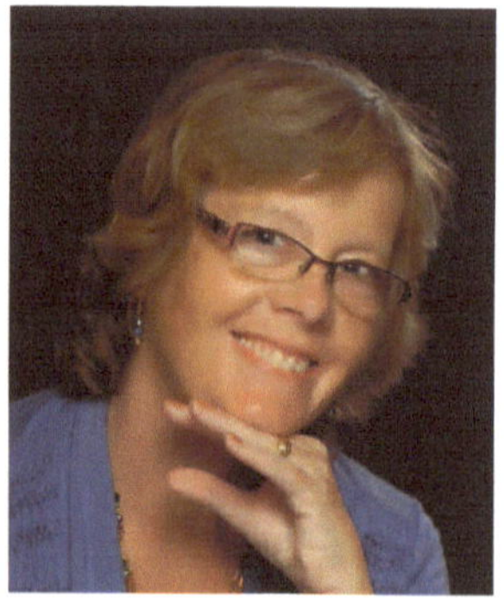

I have been painting since I was ten years old. Painting pet portraits is a self-indulgent activity because nothing gives me more pleasure than looking into the eyes of an animal. I am presently appreciating the process of creating a program for traumatized youth who will be paired with shelter dogs. My passion for animals competes with my passion for painting.

www.JanDawsonArtist.ca

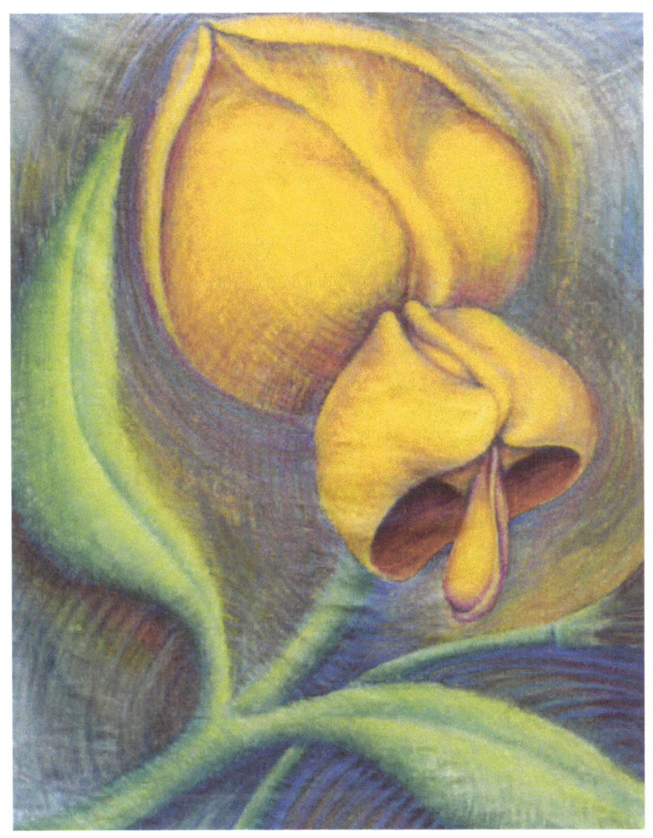

Broom Flower
Jan Dawson
43x38
Acrylic/oil pastel

This painting holds within its folds, that exuberant, mysterious lust that I was feeling in every cell of my being when I'd just met the man who was to become my husband.

Jan Little

Jan Little is a Penticton artist known for her whimsical paintings and illustrations of local flora, fauna and friends. A graduate of Emily Carr University, she has spent the last 15 years working as an illustrator, graphic designer, painter and sculptor. Her work seeks to reveal the layers of reality and magic in the beautiful and funny world she sees herself in. Erotic art has been a secret passion that she has never shared before now…

www.facebook.com/JanLittleArt

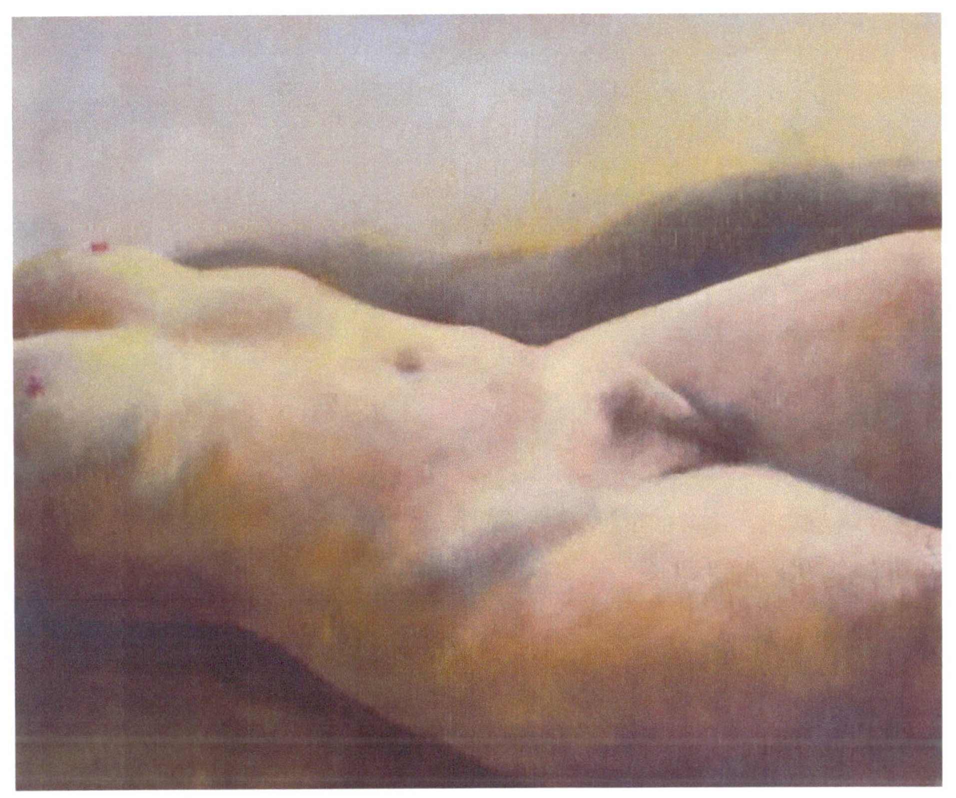

Overexposure
Jan Little
8x10
Acrylic on panel

I've been wanting to open up to you…

Jennifer Burrows

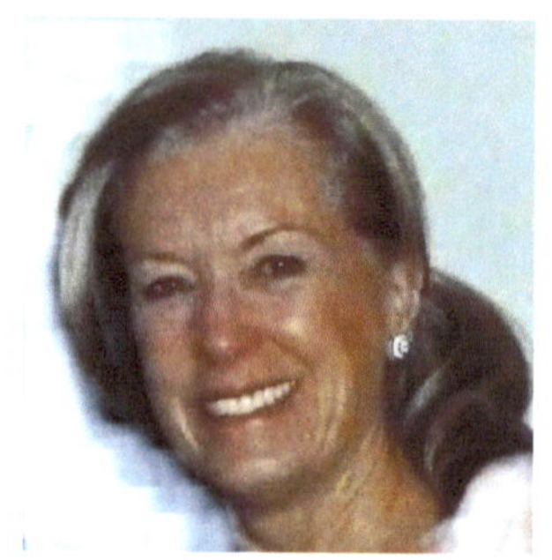

Optimism inspires me as do people, places and things that are courageous and unique. I feel most alive and inspired when outdoors, in particular when I'm near the ocean or when hiking land that I know and love. In these undisturbed spaces I sense life everywhere, and this strengthens my desire to paint with the same sense of awe and freedom I feel in nature. I see art being similar to life: each as a series of adventures containing unexpected elements, twinges of mystery and many unanswered questions.

www.JenniferBurrowsArt.com

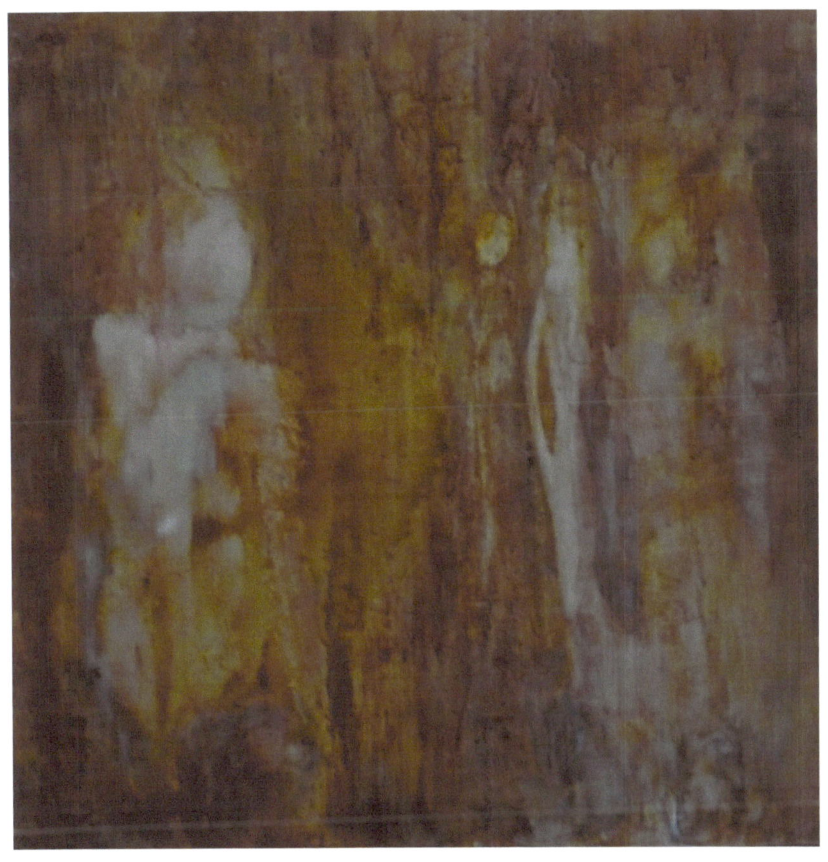

Sisterhood
Jennifer Burrows
36x36
Acrylic on Canvas

The women never speak of meeting in the clearing or of the intimacies revealed

Jessika LaFramboise

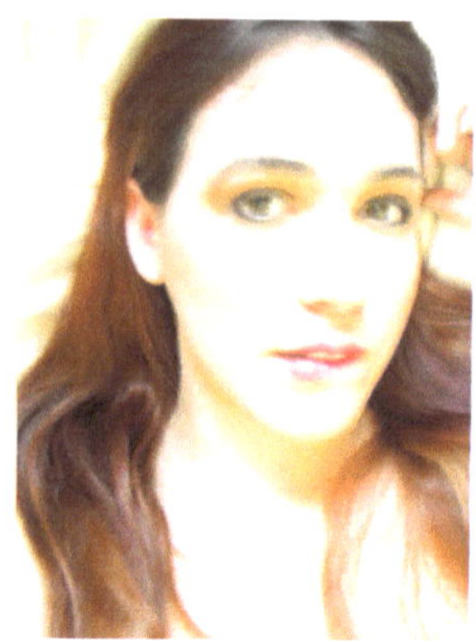

Born and raised in British Columbia, and further schooled in Alberta, Jessika is a not-so-closeted exhibitionist. Completely and utterly unhappy with her body, she forces herself to see it through art. She uses and abuses her art in order to taste, to touch, to tease. She likes to question the difference between art and erotica, art and sex, art and pornography. She wants you to see her, what is really her. Her life force. Her womanhood. Her centre. Her… vagina.

www.theatre86.com

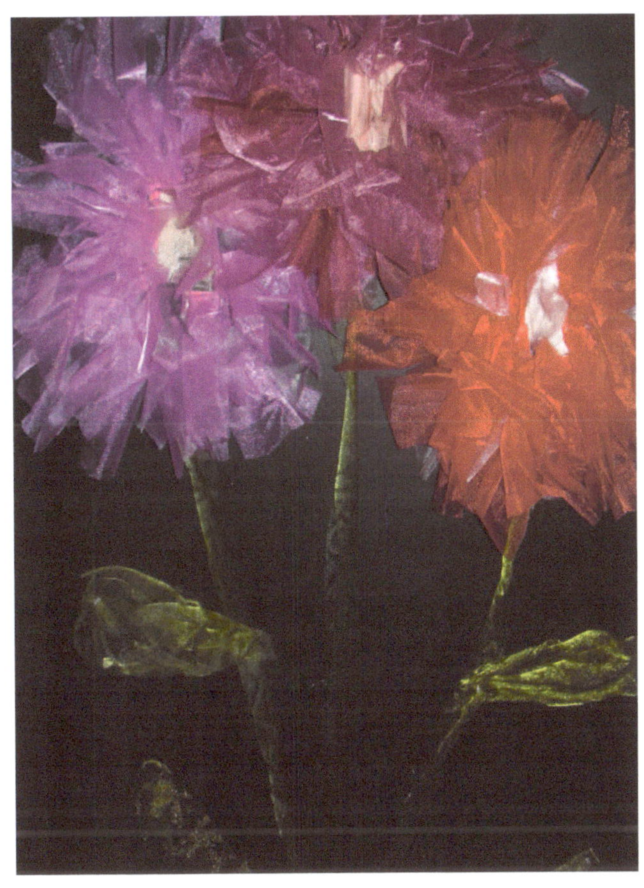

Secret Garden
Jessika LaFramboise
6'x2'
Tulle and Photography (3D interactive piece)

Take a peek inside her most secret of gardens.

Johann Wessels

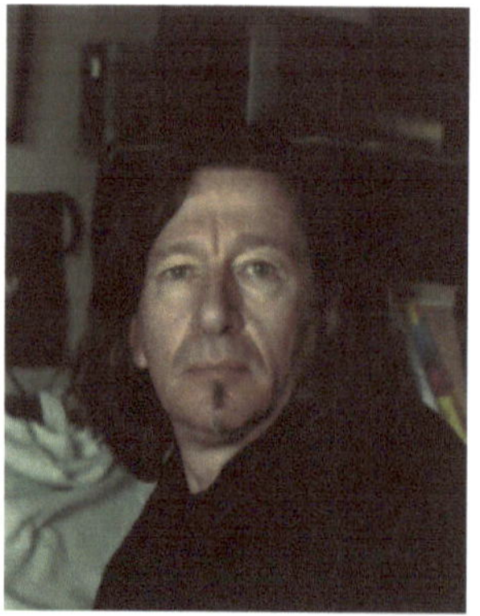

I see the Okanagan Lake every day. I swim in it often. The feeling evokes memories that reach back to my earliest recollections of water on my skin. I make art all the time. I cook when I am not making art. Sensory experiences are vital to my existence.

www.JohannWessels.com

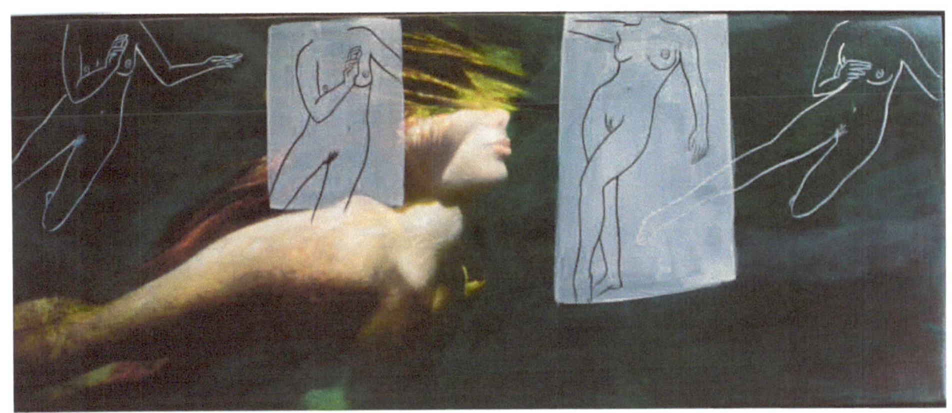

Submerge
Johann Wessels
18x44
Digital print with acrylic paint

You feel the water's embrace all over your skin as the sun paints dancing lines of warmth on it.

Julia Trops

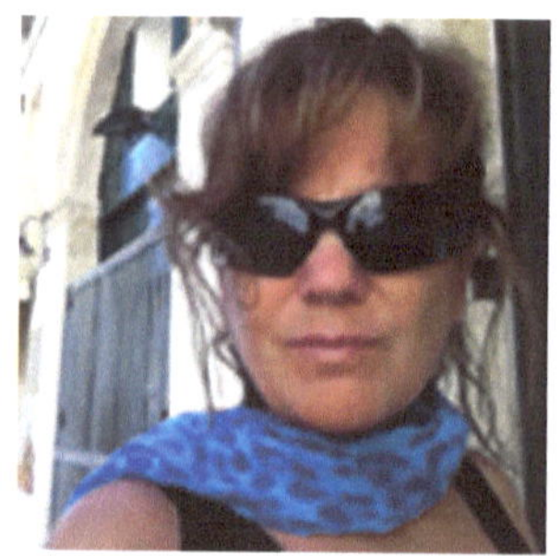

I'm living the dream I've had for lifetimes. Artist, writer, freedom fighter, animal advocate, not too good under authoritarian types, I like to do what I want. I'm a bit of a geek and I'm okay with that.

www.JuliaTrops.com
www.VenusIsRising.com

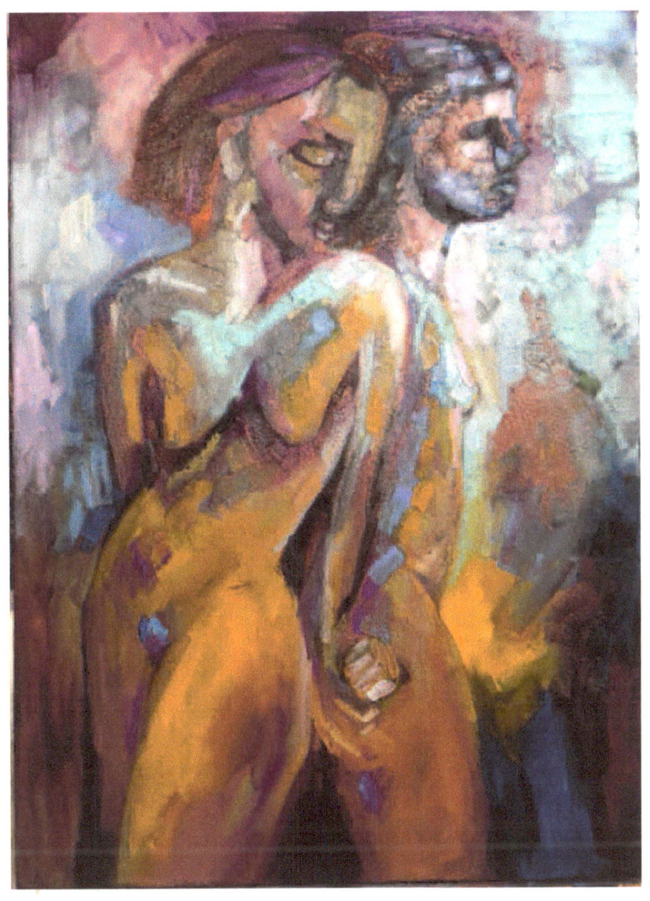

Love Story
Julia Trops
30x24
Oil on canvas

From the minute of my first whispered love story, I started looking for you (from Rumi)

Julie-Ann Miller

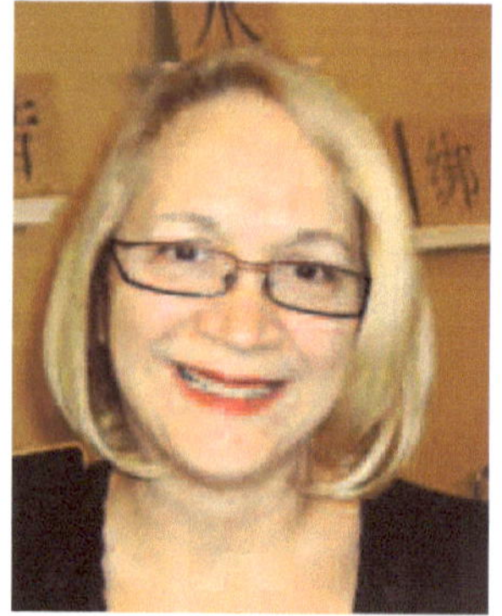

Julie-Ann Miller's work in human services has made her an imaginative observer. Quick to see the detail and the quirky, she converts this to her figurative paintings that are alive in vibrant colored moments of meaning. Julie-Ann has enjoyed living in Penticton and capturing moments in paint for 6 years. A member of the Lake-to-Lake Studio Tour group and an active member of the South Okanagan Similkameen Chapter of the Canadian Federation of Artists.

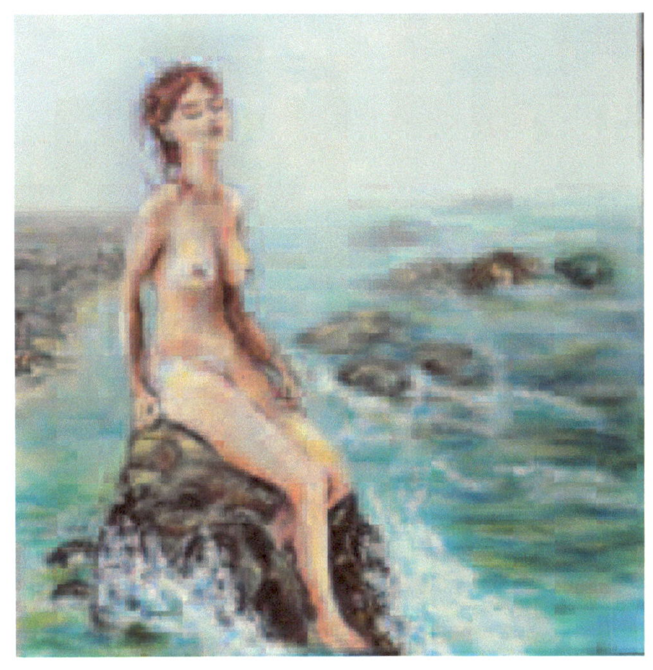

Remembering
Julie-Ann Miller
20x20
Acrylic on canvas

Is it a siren's call or a forgotten past?

June Seed

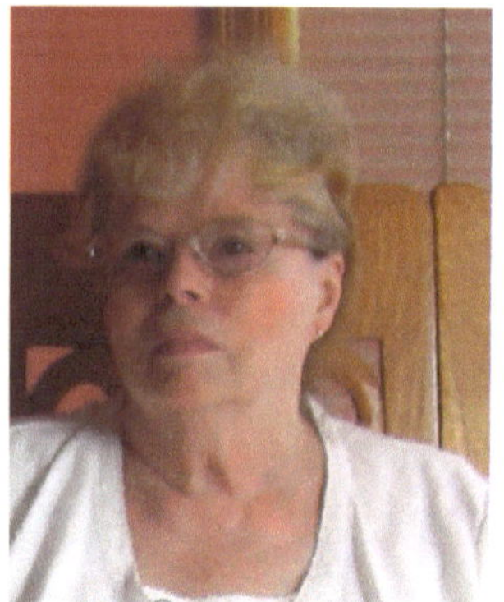

Art has been my passion ever since I was old enough to draw. It's many years later and much gnashing of teeth, but all the schooling and practice have led me to my place in art. While I have painted in all mediums I have come to rest with acrylics, inks and oils, to develop free form abstracts that convey a mood or a sense of happening. I have been a strong supporter of the arts at the community level and exhibited and sold my work.

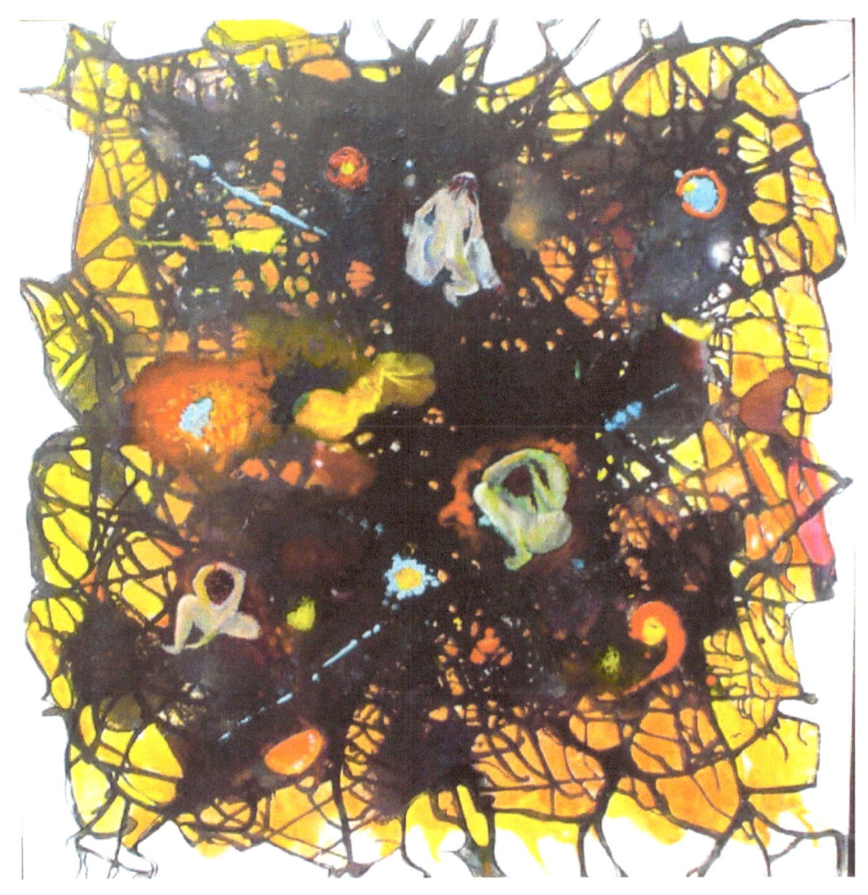

Sensual Forms
June Seed
38x38
Mixed Media, Acrylic and Ink on Canvas

In the existence of desire there is no peace

Keith Funk

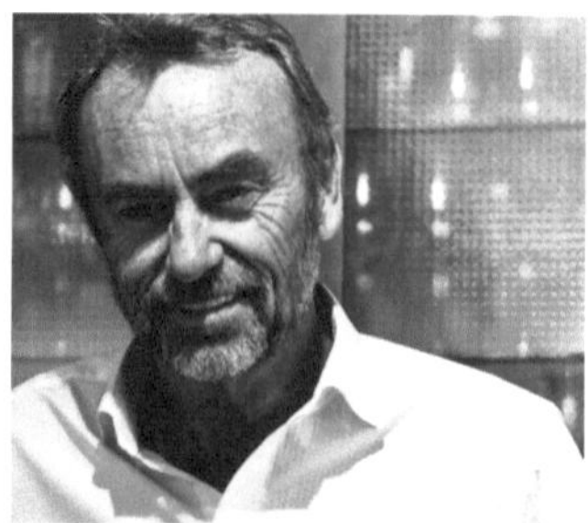

Keith graduated with a degree in Fine Arts in 1970. He has painted continually while also pursuing creative interests in Architecture, Urban Planning and Urban Design, completing his Masters in Architecture in 1990. Overall, the expression and products in all fields of design have been a continuous exploration of imagination, social relevance and a desire to add meaning through creative expression. Keith paints daily at his studio in Kelowna and has sold and marketed his work to clients in Canada, USA and Europe.

www.StudioFunkArt.com

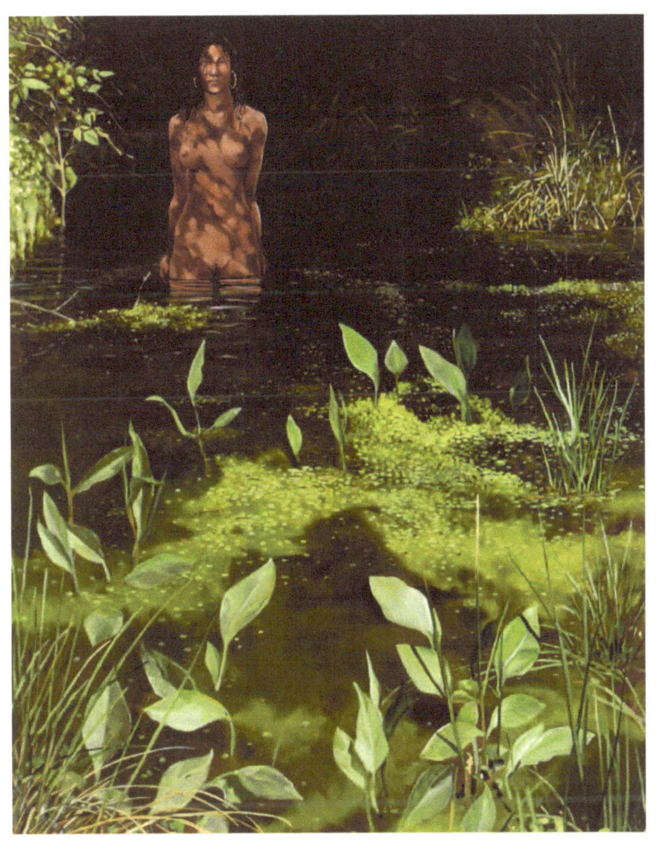

Innocence Abandoned
Keith Funk
48x60
Oil on canvas

Nature dominates this work as the figure emerges unshielded on the verge of innocence lost.

Kena Cumming Cormier

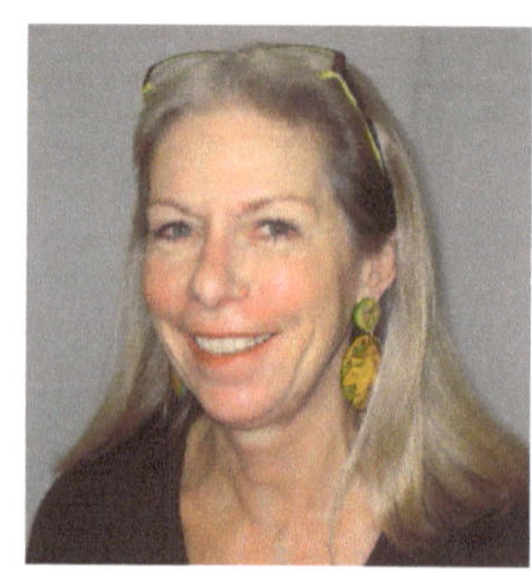

Living in the Okanagan most of her life, Kena was born in Penticton in 1952, no plans of returning, but life's like that & she did in 1997. Art has played a major role in her life & attending the Fine Arts program, at the Kelowna campus of OK College in the 70's confirmed that it always will. Currently, she & husband Lawrence share a workshop at their home gallery/sculpture garden/B&B, Cormier's Studio. Please drop by to visit...... they are open most days 11 -5pm.

www.CormierStudio.com

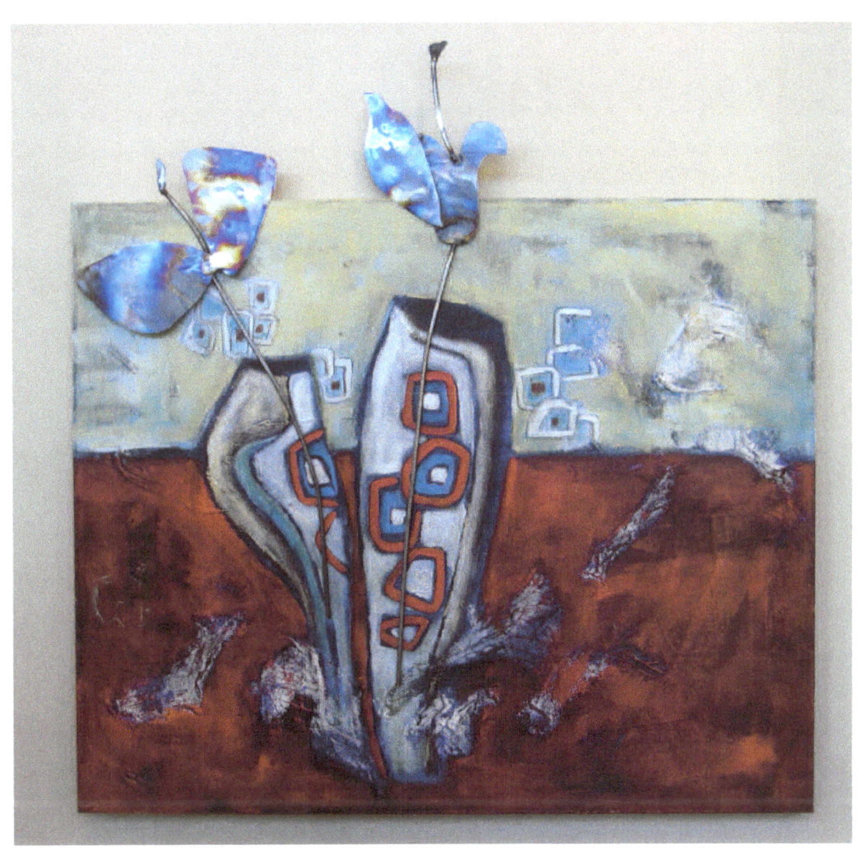

Chrysalis
Kena Cumming Cormier
30x30
Canvas, acrylic, mild steel

Don't we all dream of flying?

Kendi Clearwater

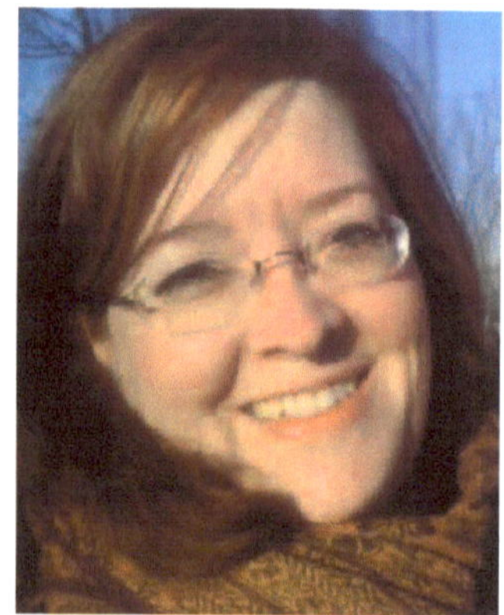

I am the daughter of Joy, mother of three amazing young women, sister to four crazy, inspiring women, and grandmother of one astounding toddler. I love the beauty of women and am inpired by the complexity of human relationships. I have now reached the age in my life where I am not afraid to own my own truth. I have a vision of what I wish to create, in images, words and song, and so, like you - I find my way. Now 51, 5 ft 6ish, I live in the Okanagan, .. the rest changes without notice.

www.ArtByKendi.com

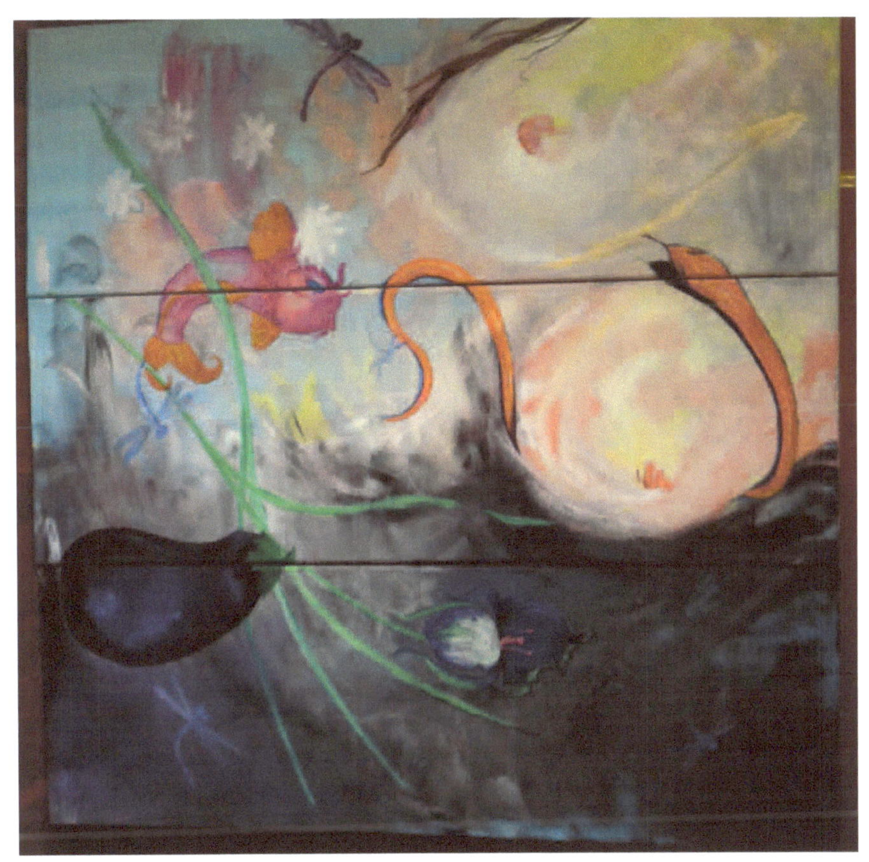

Morpheus calls
Kendi Clearwater
36x36
Acryllic

What secret desires await in our dreams?

Kim-Alan Dawson

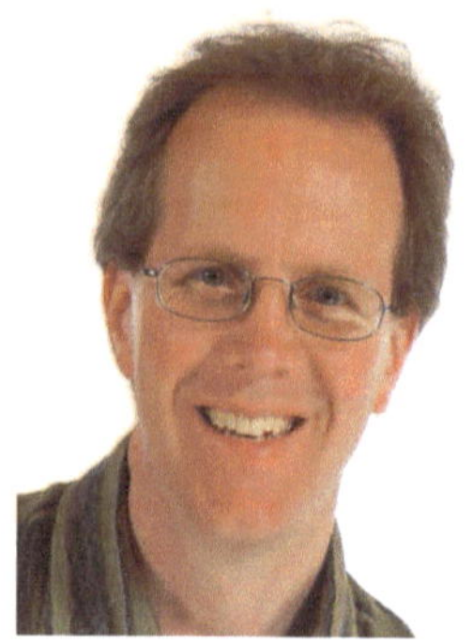

Born in Finland, I grew up in Vancouver. I have an active counselling practice in which I have helped distressed couples for the last ten years. Currently in a 21-year-long marriage, I have lived in Kelowna for the last 4 years. I enjoy hiking, spending time with our dogs, and participating in the Unitarian Fellowship of Kelowna.

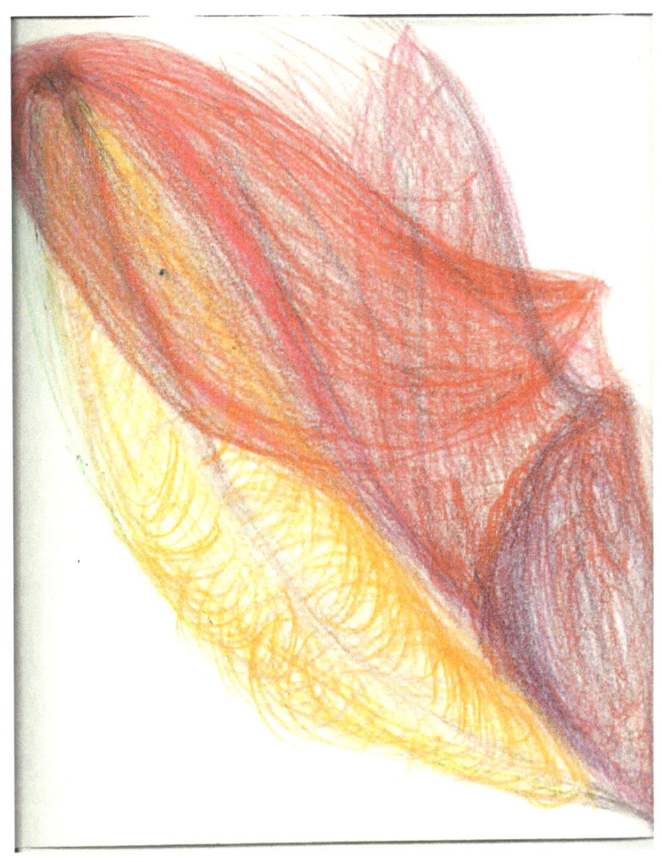

Two Peas In a Pod
Kim-Alan Dawson
10x14
Pastel

Two Peas In a Pod represents the symmetry and grace of the homoerotic

Kim Walker

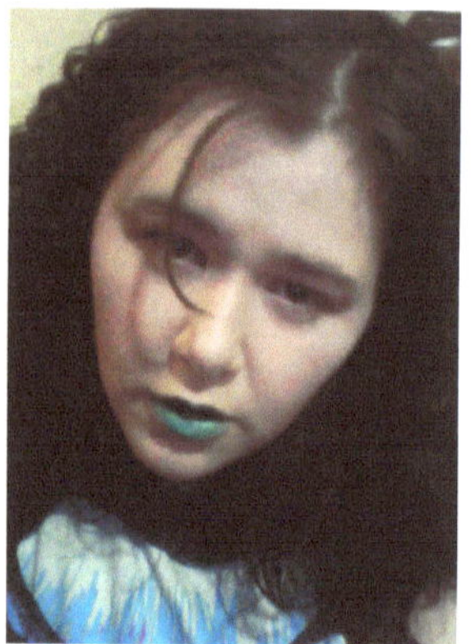

Kimberly Walker is a digital and traditional illustrator. She is heavily influenced by modern gothic fashion, 18th century Rococo interior design, and Botany. She was born, educated, and is currently living in the Okanagan Valley. She is known for her high detail ink drawings and her colourful photomanipulations.

www.LacePistol.com

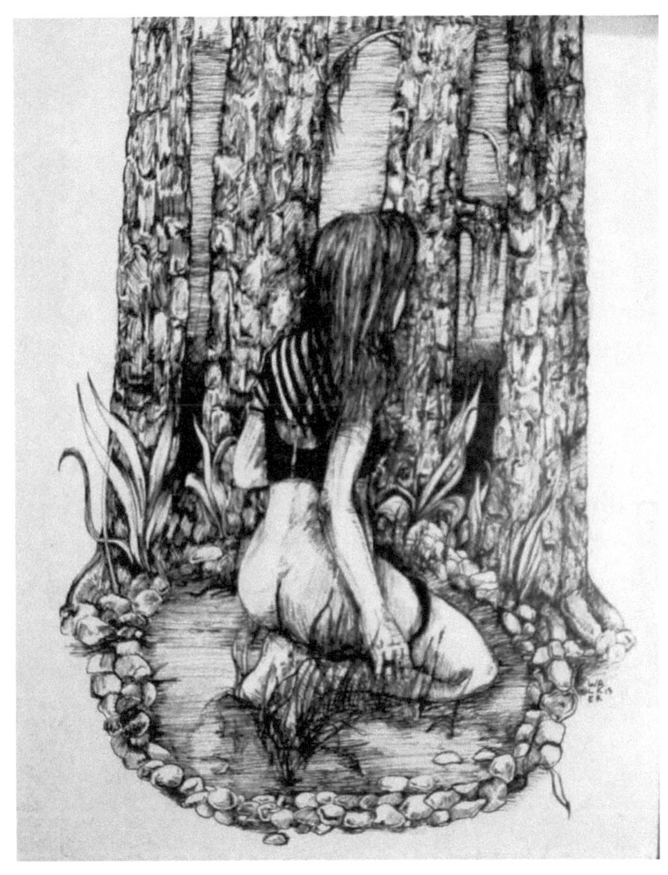

Indigo
Kim Walker
14x11
Ink

... she turned her head, waved, and said “hey”. That’s when my heart crawled into my stomach.

Krista Berrigan

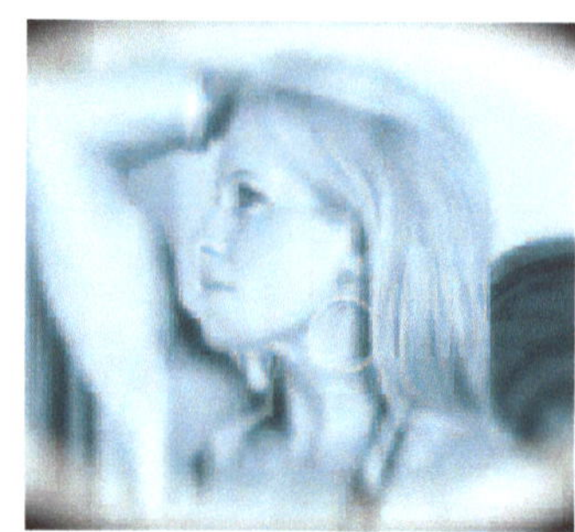

I began painting 18 years ago after I saw a beautiful abstract painting a friend had done with left over house paint. I decided I too could do this. Working with oils inspired me, it was forgiving and changeable so much fun to work with. I have painted many different abstracts on canvas. My creations are developed by my own versions and images of bodies, colors and shapes. Large canvas painting tends to be the moment now and I have moved to acrylic which births from a charcoal sketch. I find the female dimension fascinating and loves how it unfolds on canvas in its seductive interpretation and strength.

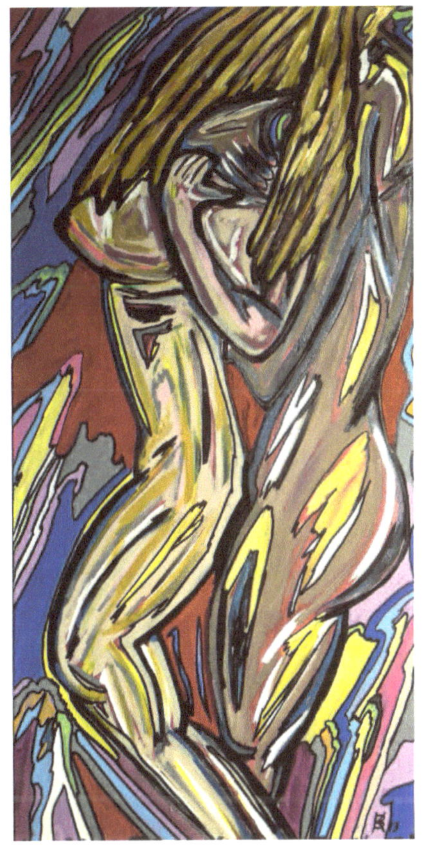

Embrace in Wonderment
Krista Berrigan
19.75x39
Acrylic on canvas

The thirst of the thrust of the embraced touch fromt the back to the front

Kristine Lee

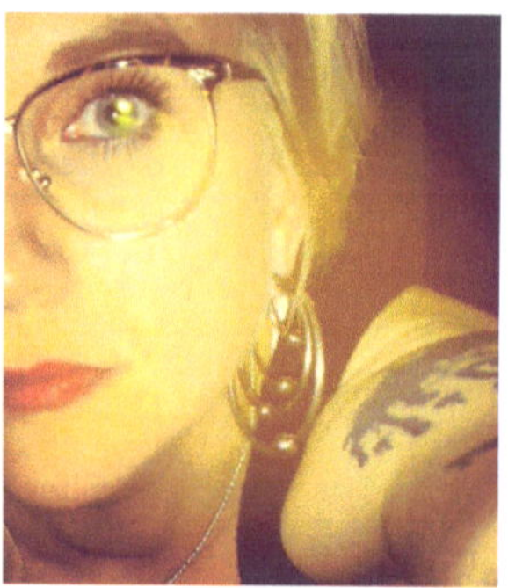

There was always 3 things I wanted to be, a mother, a wife and an artist. It wasn't until I realized that I only wanted to be a mother and an artist that I found my so called artistic mojo . My paintings and my confidence have gone hand in hand, growing and evolving. I have never been as comfortable in my own skin or with my paint brush. Since my kids and I have taken on this adventure alone I have learned to embrace it all and express it all, I live by it and paint by it.

www.Facebook.com/SmudgedPaintbyKristineLee

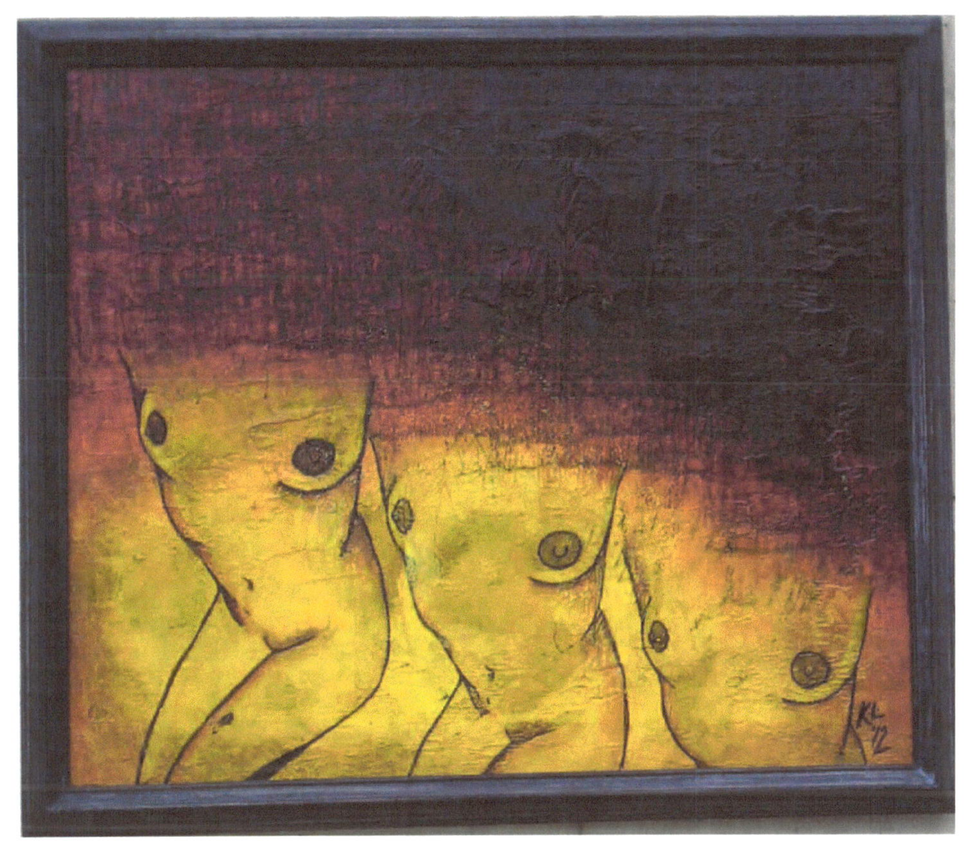

Nude 3
Kristine Lee
25.5x21.5
Framed acrylic on canva

He said he couldn't handle one of me, so I gave him three

Laurel Fredin

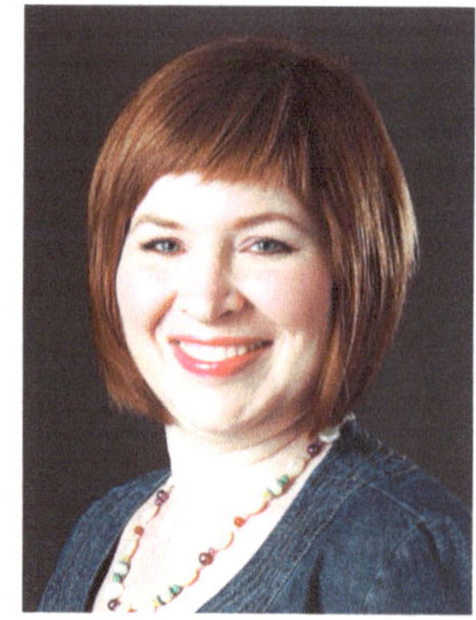

I have considered myself an artist since childhood, so it seemed natural to start my formal education with a diploma in Fine Arts. A second diploma in Graphic Design and Communications formed the foundation for my career as a designer, working for almost 20 years in a number of tremendous studios in Vancouver, BC. The years of drawing, painting and sculpting nudes though, had left a burning ember in my heart. I knew I would have to return to my true passion, so when my family and I moved to Vernon in the winter of 2008, I felt a new awakening. Working with clay, which ironically is my husband's name, has always been a home for my soul. I feel blessed to be feeding my inner need once again.

www.LaurelFredin.ca

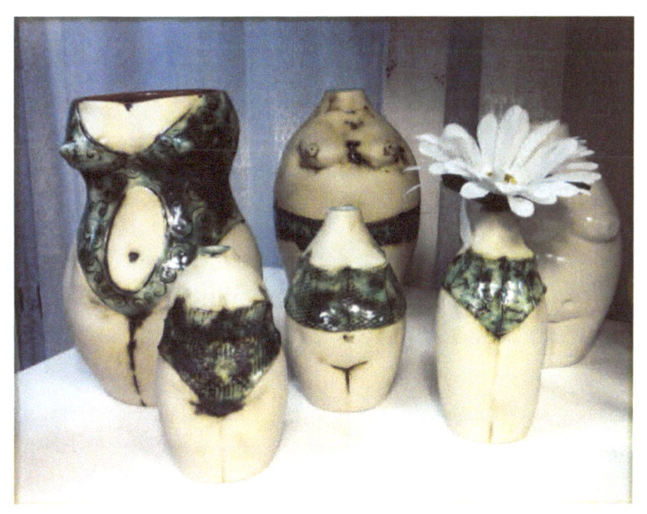

Goddess, She Loves Her Tattoos
Goddess, Wearing a Favourite Corset
Goddess, Sporting in Her Swimwear
Laurel Fredin
7x6x14
White Stoneware, Cone 6

Lawrence Cormier

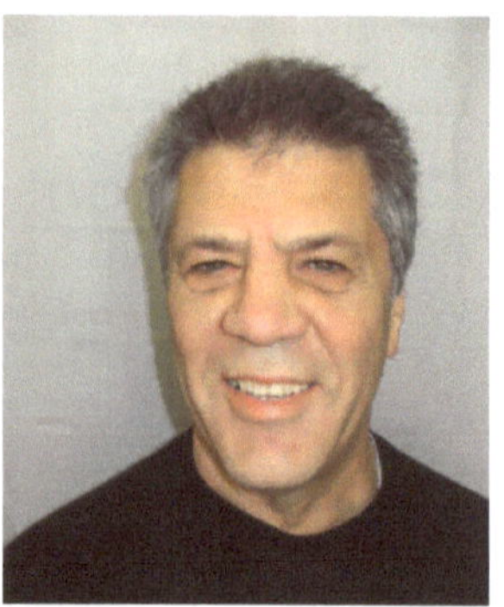

A self taught sculptor, he was born in 1948 and resided in Saskatchewan until 1988 when he wised up & moved to the Okanagan. A "hands on" fellow all his life, his philosophy has always been, "never a challenge too large to conquer". So delving into a new medium seemed a natural evolution, the beauty though this time, was for his pleasure..... to create ART. Steel is his medium of choice and he invites you to visit the "home" gallery, sculpture garden & art studio, located in Penticton BC, which he shares with his wife, Kena.

www.CormierStudio.com

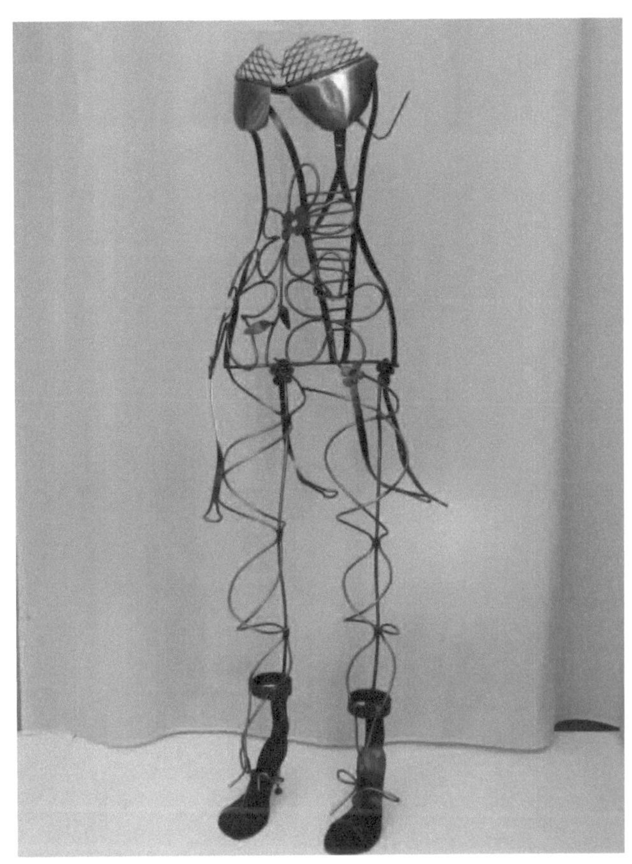

Gertie's Garters
Lawrence Cormier
5 feet x 2 feet x 2 feet
Steel

The perfect bedroom companion

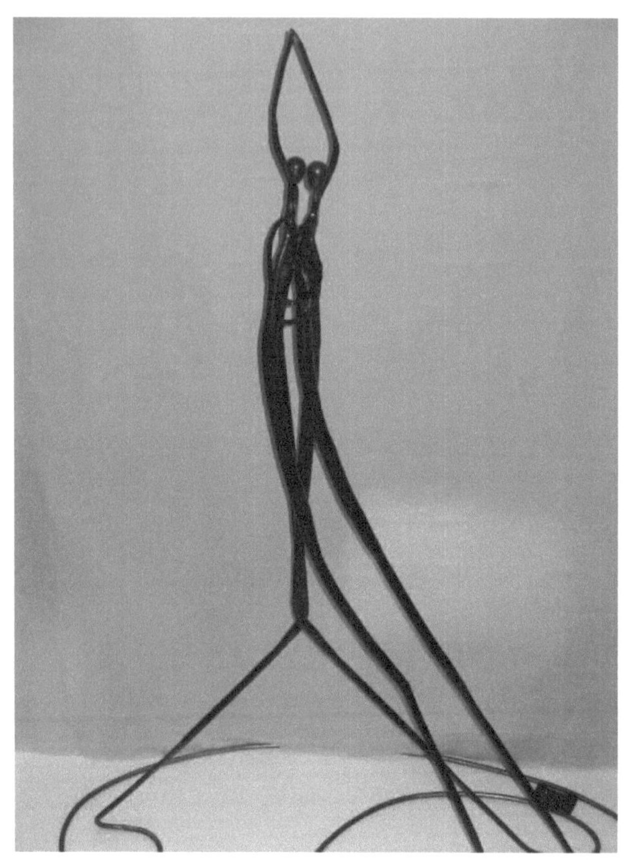

To Dance
Lawrence Cormier
5 feet x 3 feet x 2 feet
Steel

The lover's embrace of tango

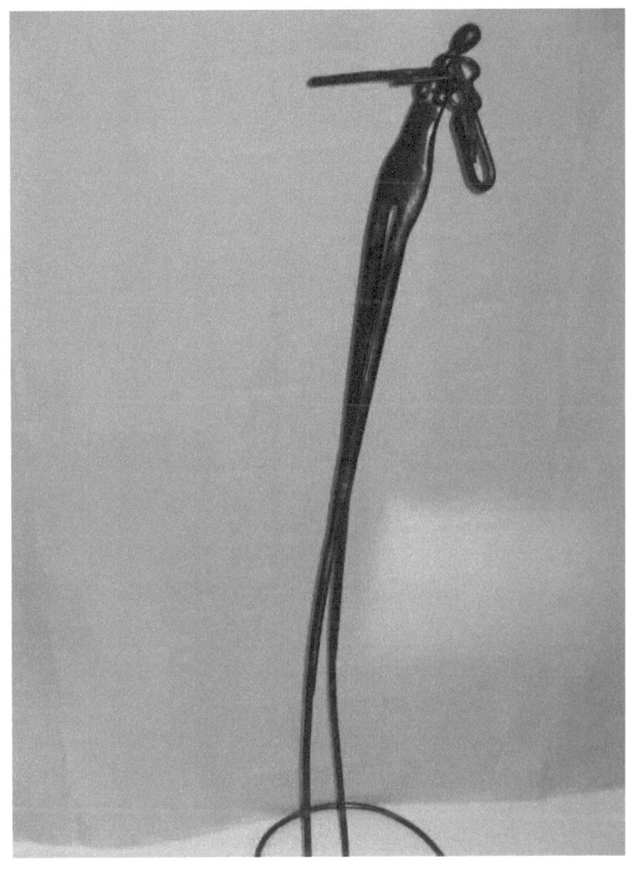

Melody
Lawrence Cormier
55x12x44
Steel

She is as sensual and soulful as the violin itself

Linda Franklin

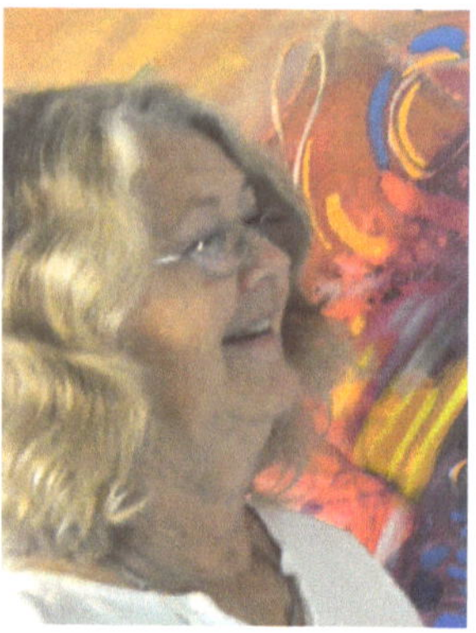

Linda Franklin was born in the Shuswap to a family of landscape painters. She was involved in making art from childhood, at the easel of her grandfather and her uncle, and later at the Art Gallery of Victoria. She studied fine arts in England and Canada. For the last ten years, Linda has been a blue-water sailor and returns to the Shuswap each year with new eyes. She has a lakeside home with the ever-present view of Mt. Ida, where she has her architectural design studio. She is the mother of three and grandmother of six, all of whom have returned to live in the Shuswap.

www.lazuline.ca

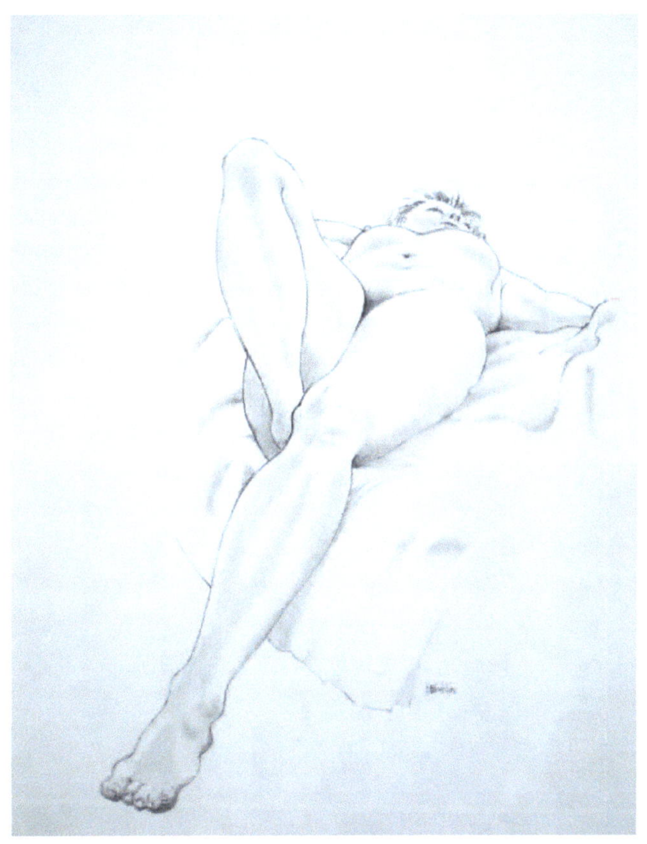

Day Dream
Linda Franklin
16x20
Graphite

Lying here, content........time to ponder and daydream

Lisa Figueroa

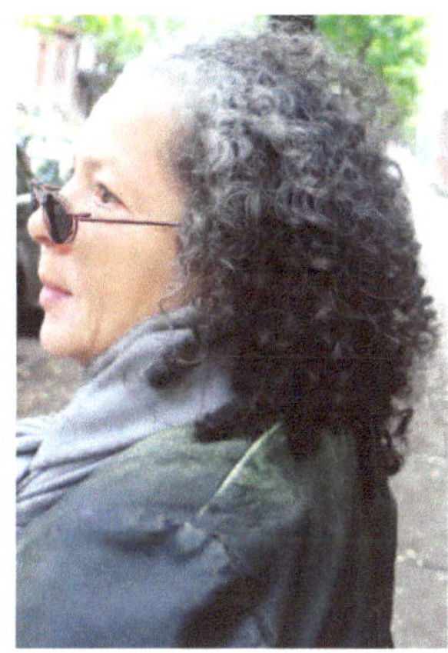

Growing up in Toronto, Lisa Figueroa enjoyed the access to life drawing for hours on Sunday afternoons at the Toronto School of Art. She was particularly fond of the "Canadian Room" at the Art Gallery of Ontario where, as a young adult, she could visit her favourite Canadian artists. At the age of 21, Lisa travelled by train to BC for a wedding. Lisa moved to the Shuswap shortly thereafter when the mountains, lakes, rivers and evergreens of this place dominated her thoughts. The colours and movement of the Shuswap are full participants in her finished imagery, that is rich with design and vibrancy. Lisa works at her studio on the lower level of the Arts Centre in Salmon Arm, and lives in Sicamous with her husband and two teenage sons in a cedar shingled home that hugs the mountainside and dips toward the water.

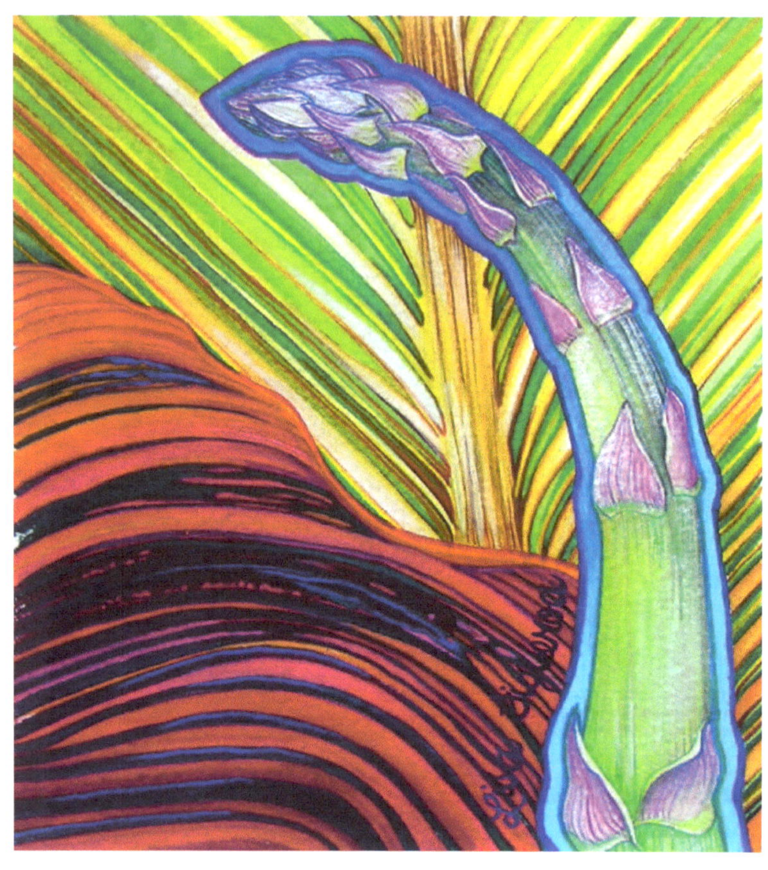

A-Spare-Guy 1
Lisa Figueroa
14x14
Water media and pencil crayons

Firm...and personality too!

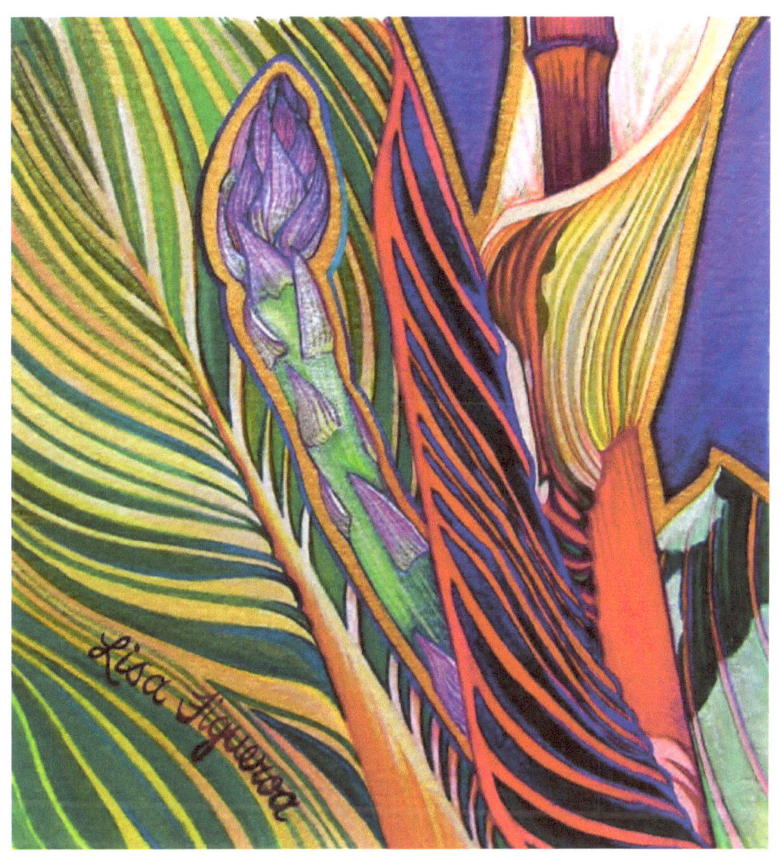

A-Spare-Guy 2
Lisa Figueroa
14x14
Water media and pencil crayons

Delicious, dangerous, sensual pleasure

Lynn Erin

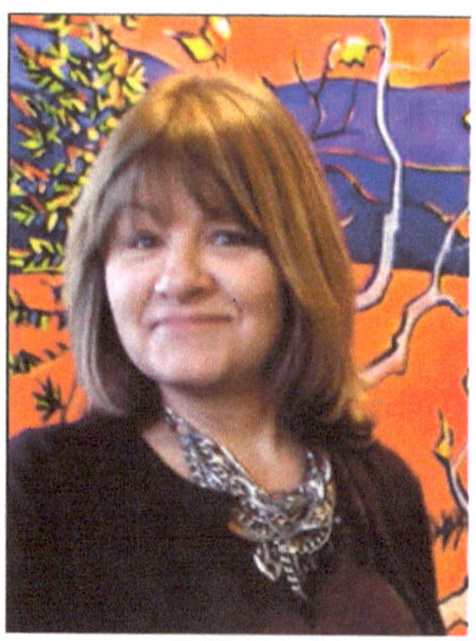

Being a woman and a mother, Lynn has naturally paid homage to the great Mother by honouring the cyclical connections between herself, her family, her work, the Earth and Universe. At 52, during this time in history, she is prepared for changes. She expects great new powers as our human culture awakens! If you know Lynn's independent activist spirit, one may be better able to see the sacred …and the silly that emanate from her heart and her art, both often evoking emotion in a most primal way. Infused with a natural sense of humour, Lynn comes across at once contemplative, profound, and playful. Bold vivid, and unique, rarely delicate, Lynn's signature style, is clear in her acrylic paintings and sculptural pieces.

www.LynnErin.com

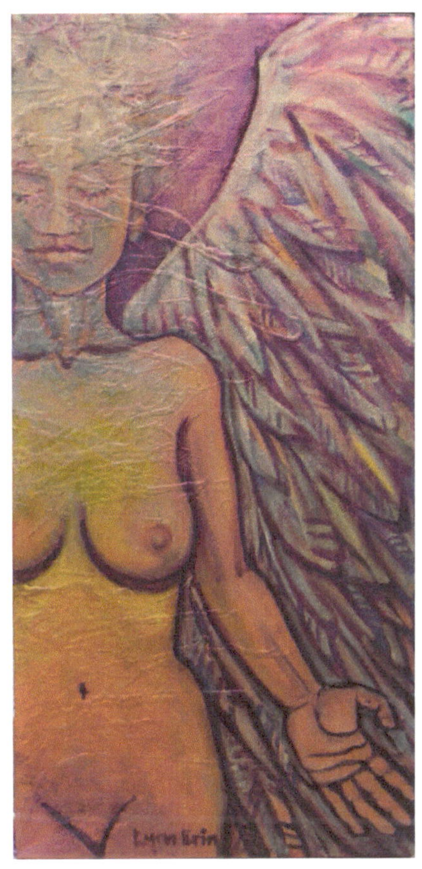

Chakras
Lynn Erin
16x8
Framed Acrylic on Canvas

Absolute Unspoken Secrets

Margot

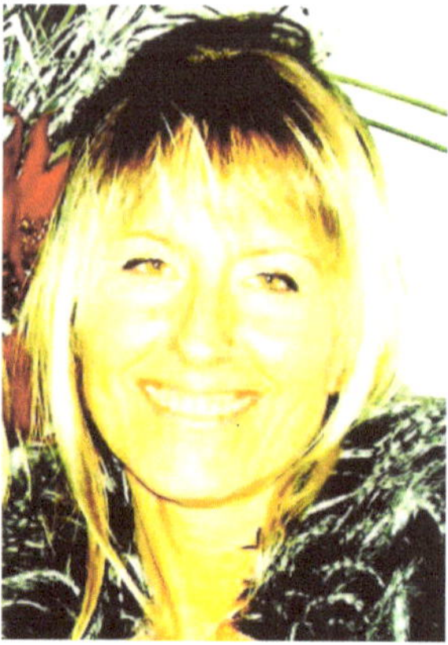

Margot, BFA, BEd, is a Vancouver born, multi-disciplinary encaustic artist. Recently mentored by Canadian internationally renowned artists Peter von Tiesenhausen and Sarah Anne Johnson, while artist-in-residence at the 2012 Toni Onley Artist Project/Island Mountain Arts School, Wells, BC. Her work is inspired by mixed media artist/author Nick Bantock and by encaustic artists Tony Sherman and Jasper Johns. Although, a BC certified art teacher, she has returned full time to her first love, making art.

www.MargotStudio.ca

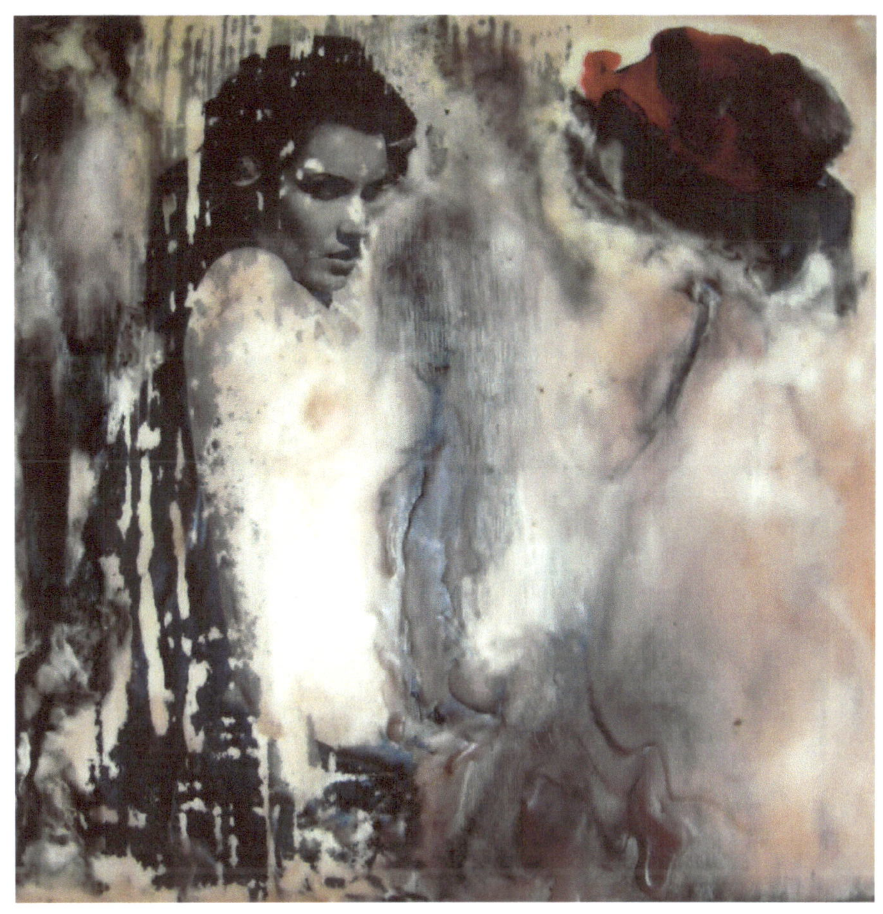

Dripping Desire
Margot
20x20
Encaustic, phototransfer & gold leaf on birch wood panel

A velvety red rose, low-rise jeans, seductive pose...dripping with desire

Photo courtesy of Eric Simard (model Hailey Winkelaar)

Mario Vucinovec

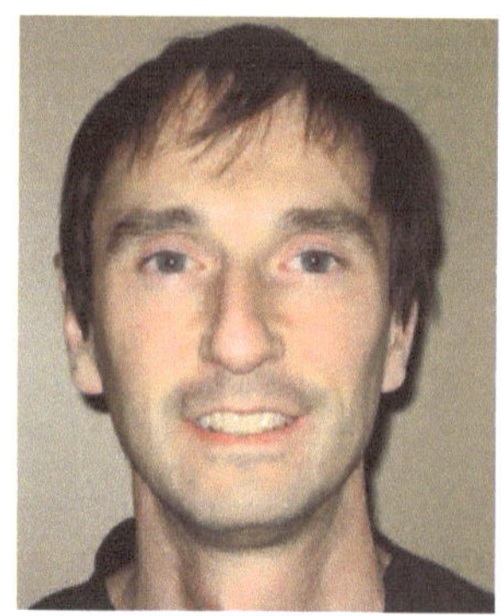

I reside in Peachland, BC, Canada after born in the former Yugoslavia and consider interpersonal relationships and all hunts convenient to luxuries as accidental history bound in human migration. While acquiring a degree in Fine Arts, my work embodies reflection on this condition; affecting the self…persons… conditions of life…occasion. All hunts for luxuries of convenience, unless witnessed alone in front of a mirror, continue to be considered inconvenient in today's modernity. …and develops artifice to persuade accidental history as products of one self.

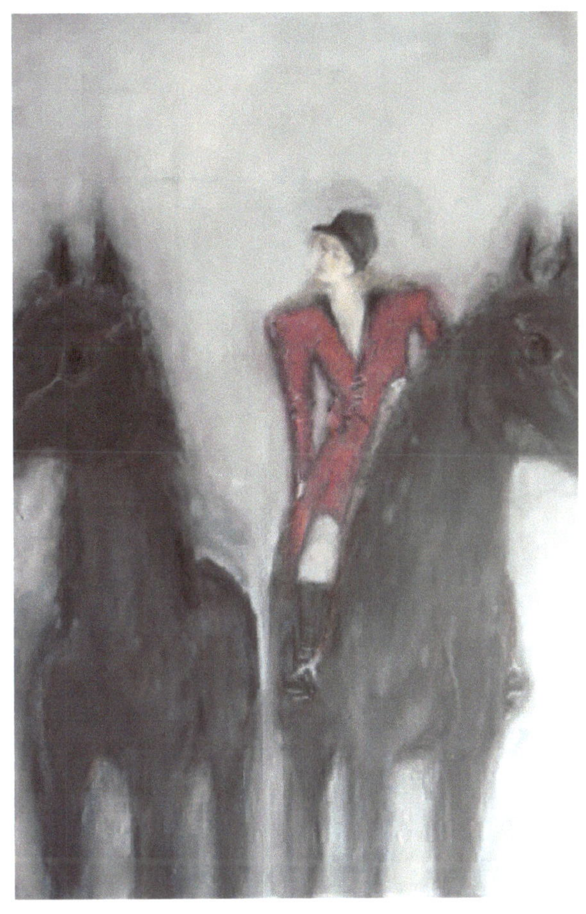

Breech
Mario Vucinovec
2'x3'
Mixed media on canvas

In turn, rocking back on her heels, each position left her shuddering.

Marissa Brown & Avery DeRousie

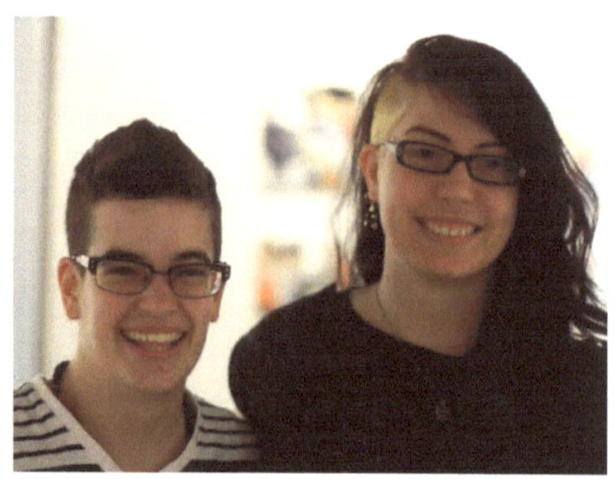

Avery & Marissa are artists from the Okanagan who first met through a desire to study & practice art. They are alumni of the BFA program at UBC's Okanagan campus and have been partners in life, love and creativity ever since.

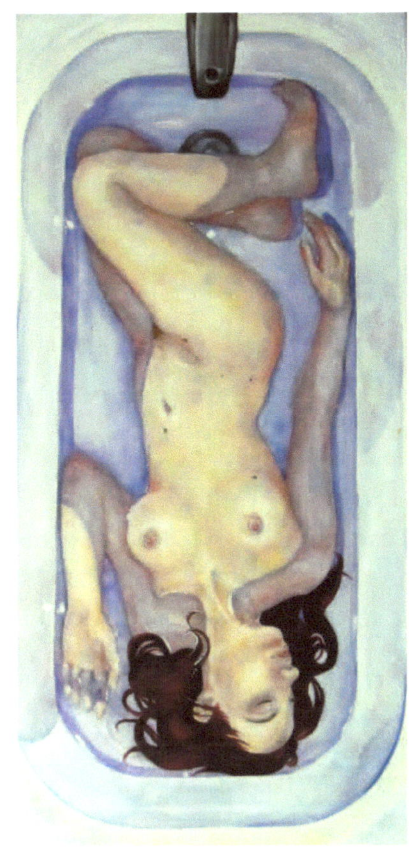

Submerge & Immerse
Marissa Brown & Avery DeRousie
18x36
Acrylic on canvas

As the facade washes away,
what is left but the desire to be immersed in secrets that are submerged below the surface?

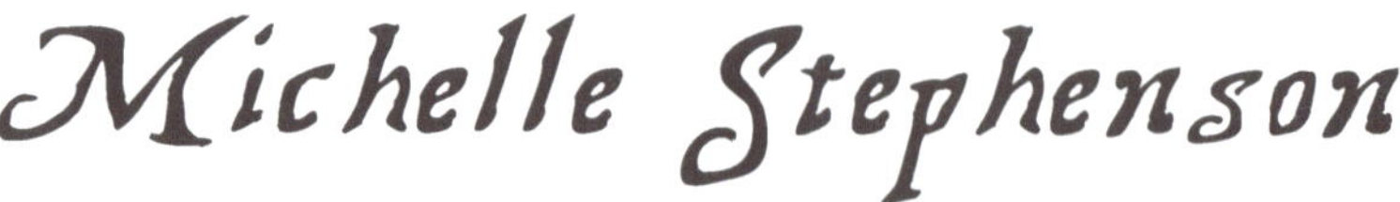

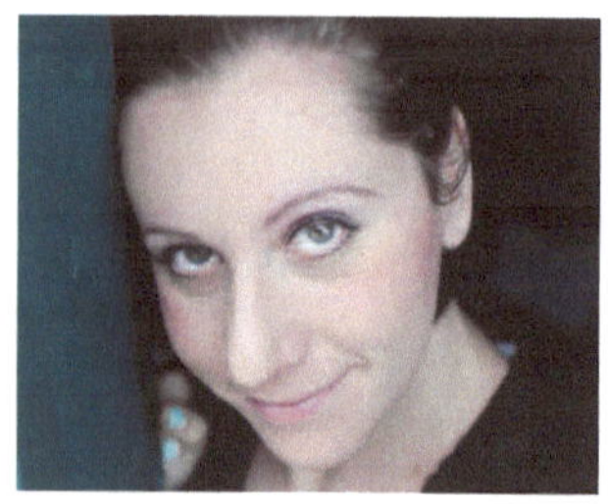

Michelle Stephenson is a local Kelowna artist. She delights in cuddle time with her two kids, Max and Charlie. Michelle is directed by an internal compass that leads her to counselling, photography, and all matter of romance and artistry, equally. Michelle loves her husband and newly appointed business co-anchor, profusely. Michael and Michelle hope to travel to Italy one day. Michelle was a top ten finalist this year in a national women's entrepreneurial competition, the MOMpreneur Award of Excellence, 2003.

www.OkanaganPhotography.ca

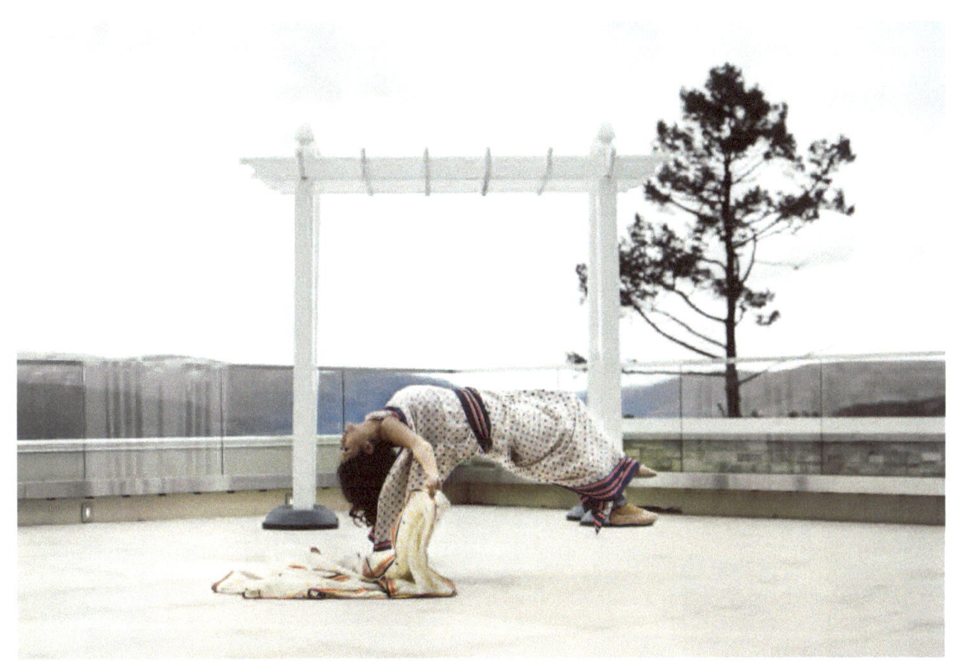

Surrender To Me
Michelle Stephenson
40x30
Photography

No purpose withstanding

Nicholas Vincent

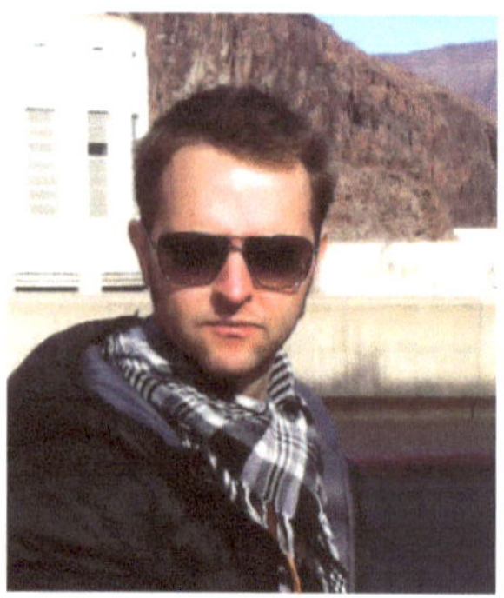

I am the rope artist and the photographer. The sensation of restraint created by the rope, brings abandonment and a relinquishing of the day-to-day. The rope becomes an object of concentrative meditation, heightening sensation and awareness, harmonizing your mind and body. Never to be forgotten, rope aesthetics are integral to the ceremony, and to the pleasure of all. As an artist I am compelled to record both sides of this passionate dance. (In this series there is no post production).

www.TastyBiscuits.com

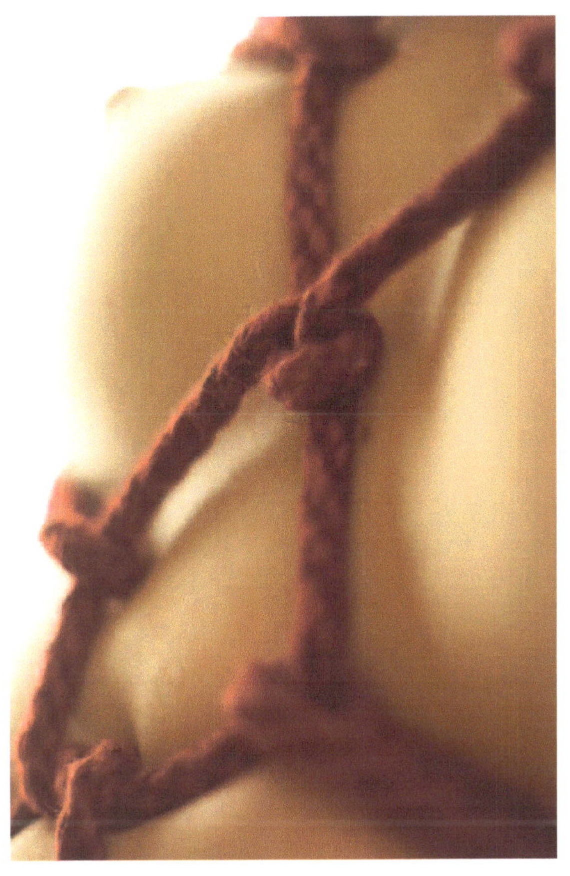

Serene Restraint 1
Nicholas Vincent
22x16
Giclee print on Art Paper (of original photograph)

Relax, you're being held, lean back, melt with the tension. Feel the embrace.

Nina Kuriloff

Nina Kuriloff has exhibited her art in galleries and colleges throughout the U.S. Her work was selected for exhibition in 25 juried competitions. One of these exhibits occurred at the Provincetown Art Association and Museum in Provincetown, MA and another took place at the Heckscher Museum of Art, in Huntington, N.Y.

www.NinaKuriloff.com

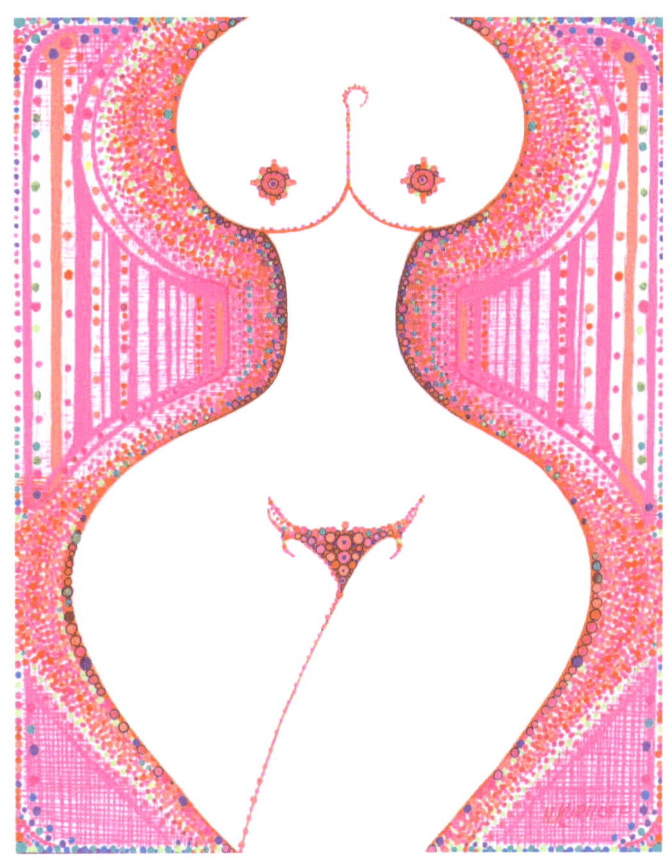

Secrets in Pink
Nina Kuriloff
10x8
Micron pens and gel pens on paper

An erotic nude woman surrounded by pink color is often secretive by nature.

Pat DeLuca

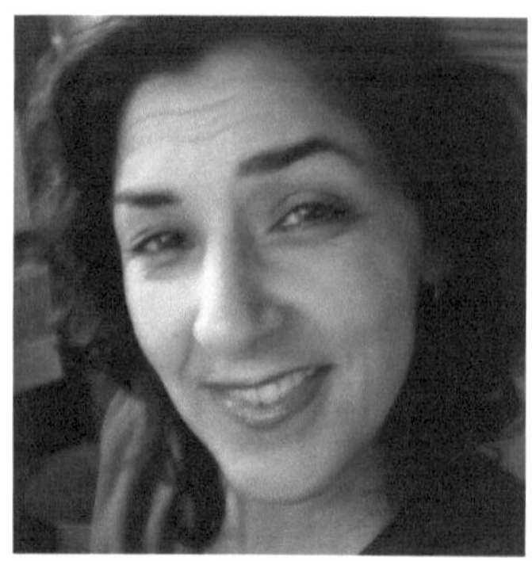

I am a middle child of six – raised by artist parents near NYC. I'm lucky. We had the privilege of playing, learning and napping in museums and galleries as soon as we were able to walk. I love to draw. I had to step away from almost everything but drawing for almost 20 years to work and raise my sons as a single parent. Three years ago, I picked up a paintbrush for the first time – to try my hand with oils and watercolors. I believe it's called "finding your medium". It's exhilarating, frustrating and next to my sons, the most gratifying thing I have ever done. Today I am the President of the New York Figure Study Guild.

www.DelucaDesign.com

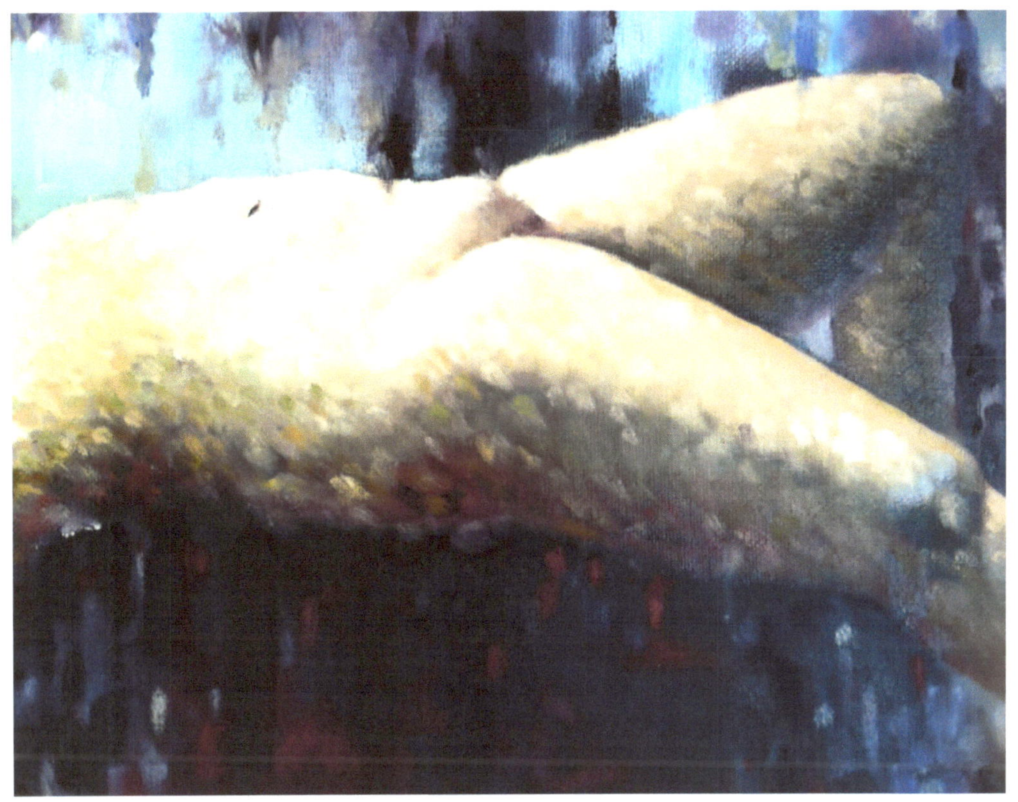

Supine
Pat DeLuca
10.5x10
Oil

The act of lying on one's back - exposed - a description of form in colour and light.

Peggy Stel

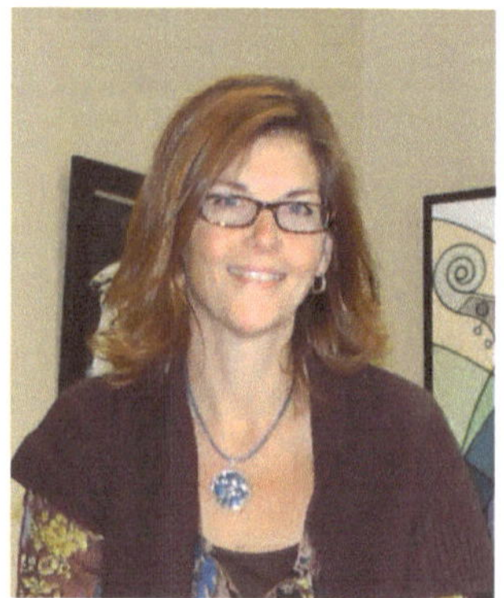

Originally from Richmond, BC, Peggy Stel majored in Fine Arts during her graduating year at Richmond High School, and was recognized with a Richmond District Award. She furthered her studies at VCC - Langara, and received a diploma in the Fine Arts Program. Peggy moved to the Okanagan in 1989, and currently resides in Penticton, BC.

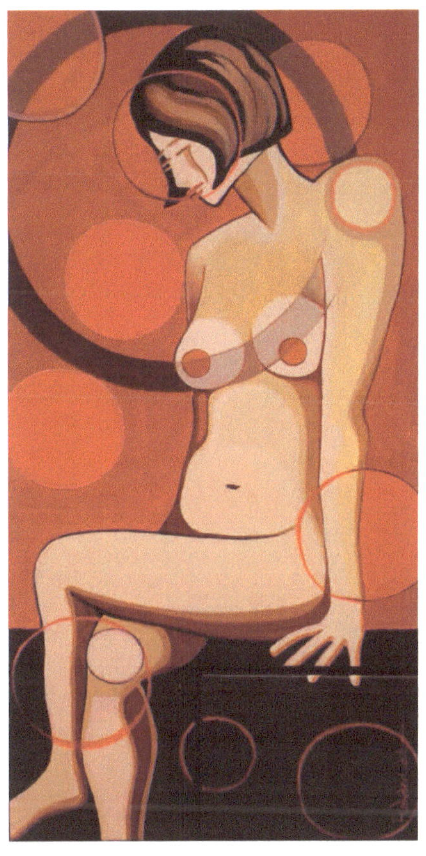

Camouflage
Peggy Stel
21.75x11.25
Acrylic on canvas

By stretching my own canvases,
I can explore different ideas and experiment with the shape and size of the canvas

Robert Canaga

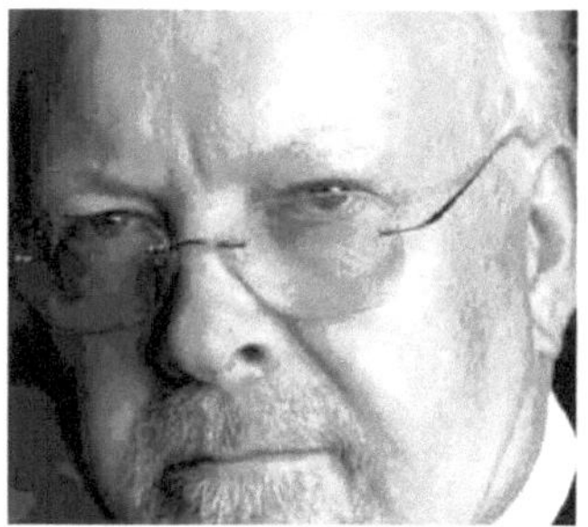

Robert Canaga, artist and art consultant, holds a Bachelor's of Arts Degree in Anthropology. When he returned from Micronesia after a summer program with the Anthropology Department at the University of Oregon, he took a drawing class thus taking a new direction into full time art. He studied printmaking for three years. He worked at the University Bookstore for over five years where he learned all he could about materials and applications, met other artists, and began to explore different mediums. He resides in Eugene, Oregon with his wife Linda and their cats. Aside from his daily studio work, he blogs about the exploration of Oregon wines, one bottle at a time.

OregonWineandMusic.blogspot.com

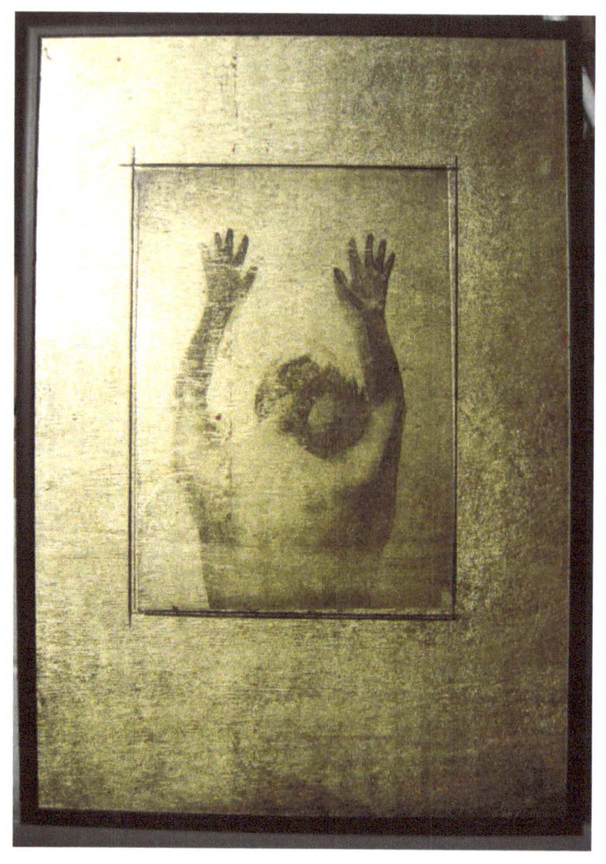

HOLD
Robert Canaga
9.25x12
Proprietary process, black inked printed directly onto wood that has been gold leafed.

Her heart raced as she pressed her nakedness into the frigid wall.

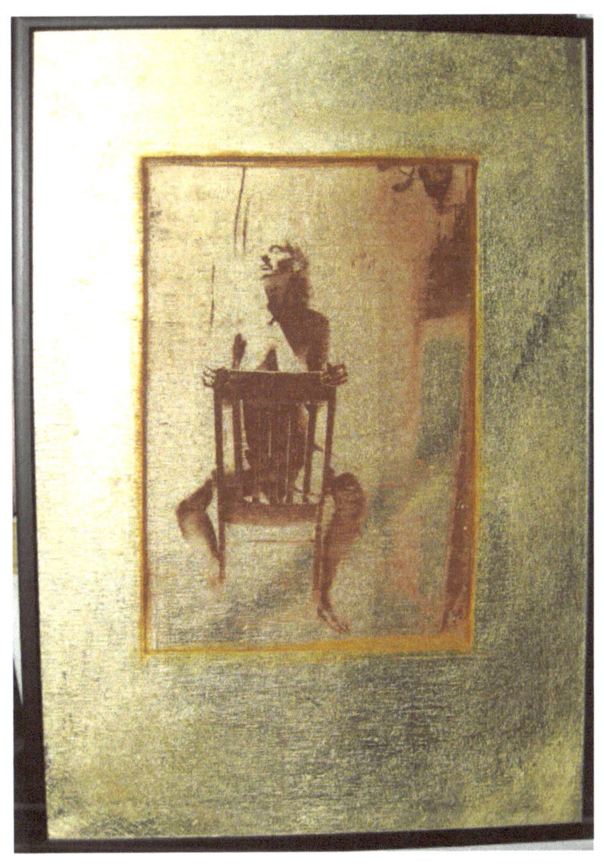

Chair
Robert Canaga
9.25x12
Proprietary process, burnt sienna printed directly onto wood that has been gold leafed

Sunlight warmed the translucent skin of her breasts.

Robert Simkins

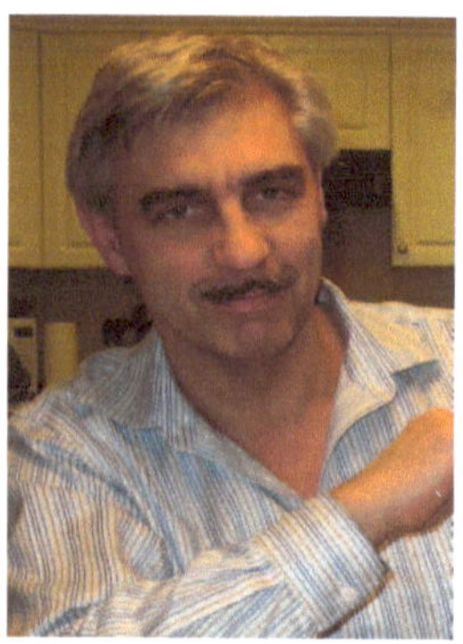

I attended Okanagan College and Vancouver College of Art (Emily Carr). After finishing my schooling I returned to the Okanagan where I worked as a carpenter. I now own Robert's Custom Framers and Gallery. This gives me a great opportunity to produce and show mine as well as other local artists work.

www.RobertsCustomFramers.ca

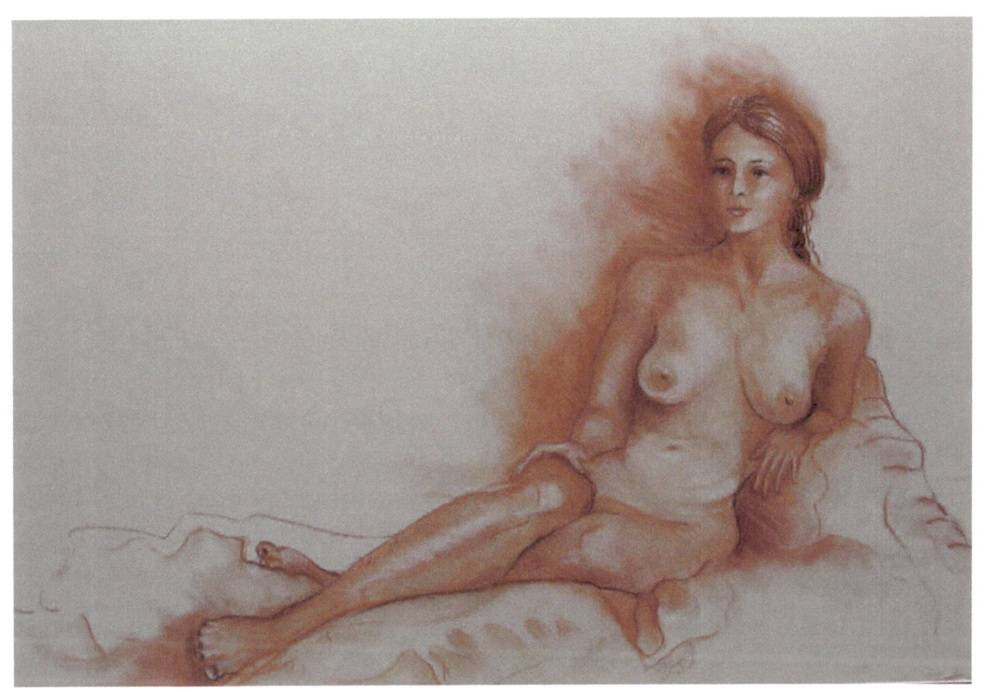

Waiting
Robert Simkins
27.5x35
Conte on illustration board

Never keep a beautiful woman waiting.

Robyn Gold

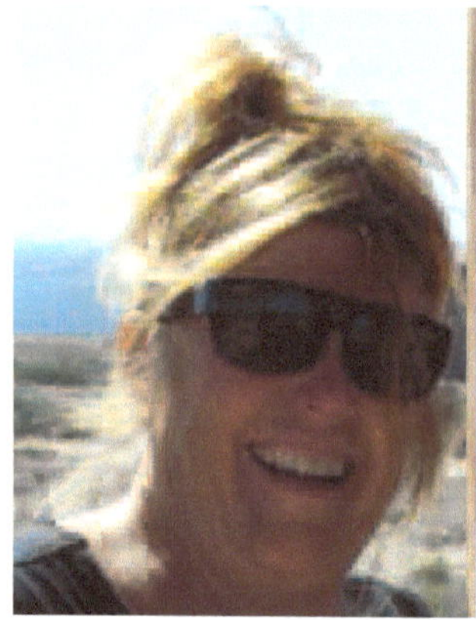

I am an emerging Visual Artist. I moved to Nelson, BC from the Okanagan. After a few years of living in the mountains surrounded by such beauty, I was inspired to pick up my brushes. I am mainly self-taught, yet have taken art many workshops from a number of talented artists. In 2012, I attended the Toni Onley Artists' Project, Wells, BC mentored by Canadian artists Peter Von Tiesenhausen and Sarah Anne Johnson. Currently, I prefer working in acrylics and mixed media. I create mainly intuitively from my soul. I believe art is an opportunity to broaden our understanding of the world around us. I currently live on my riverside acreage in Winlaw, located in the Slocan Valley.

www.RobynGold.com

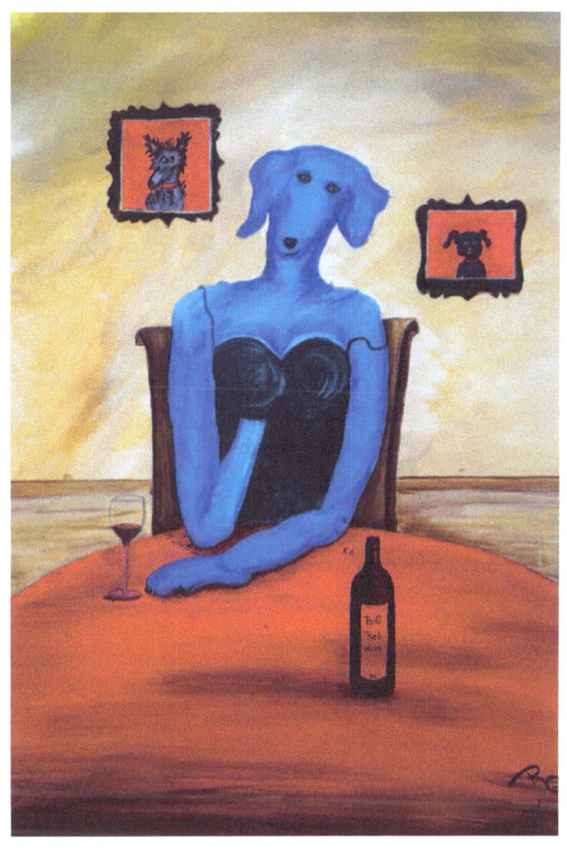

Blue Dog
Robyn Gold
24x30
Acrylic Painting

Blue Dog's wandering paw, with her faithful friends behind - keeping her "Unspoken Secrets" - while all observe.

Ron West

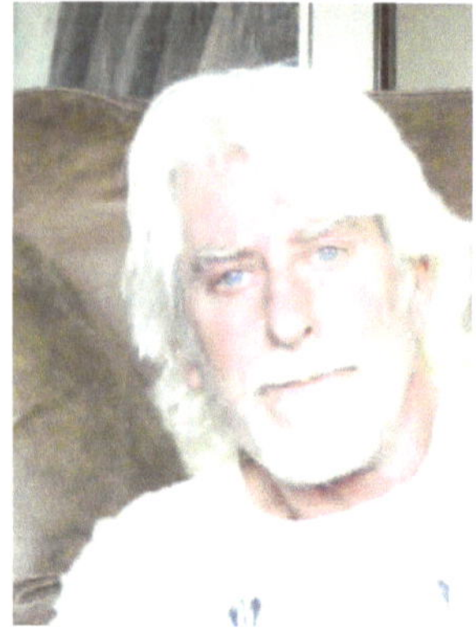

Ron is originally from Ontario, having moved out west 4 years ago. Better known for his motorcycle themed paintings he operated his own gallery before moving to the Okanagan. He is a motorcycle enthusiast and enjoys the great outdoors. Life is a great meal, eat it up!

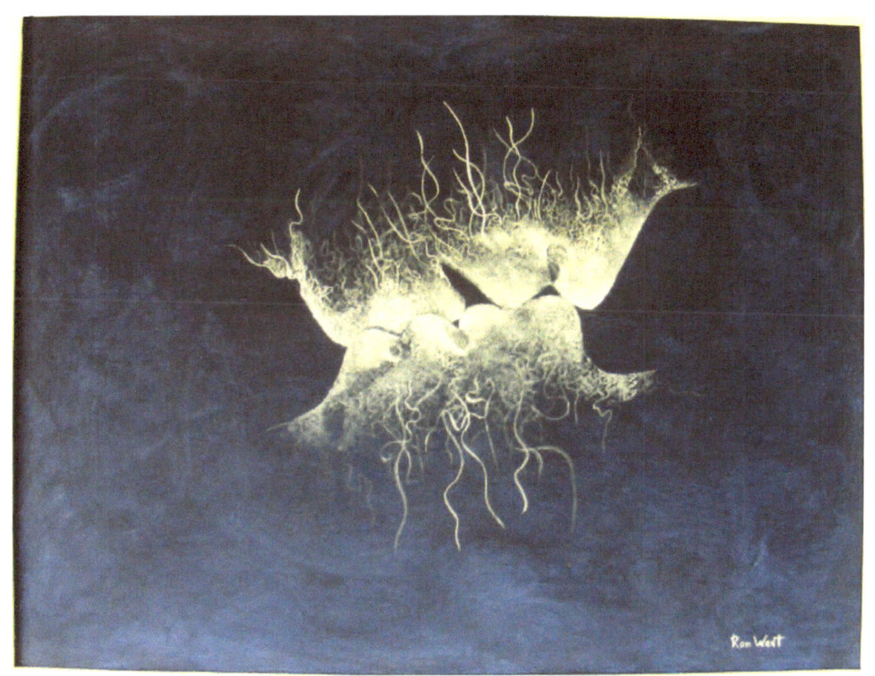

Jelly Kisshes
Ron West
29x24
Acrylic

Quiver while we flow into each other

Rory O'Neill

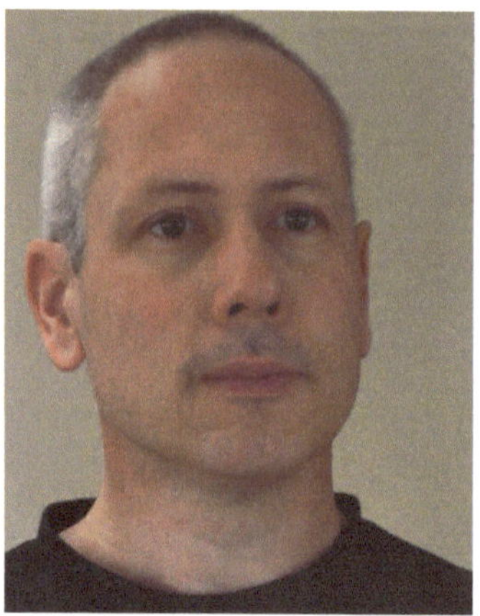

Rory O'Neill, Kelowna based sound artist, likes giving and receiving "aural". He enjoys toying with psycho-acoustics and arousing more than just the visual sensations. "Open your ears to my work. Create images in your head. I like head". He recorded sound for the Pilot and Season 1 of the L-Word... He's good at this erotic sound stuff.

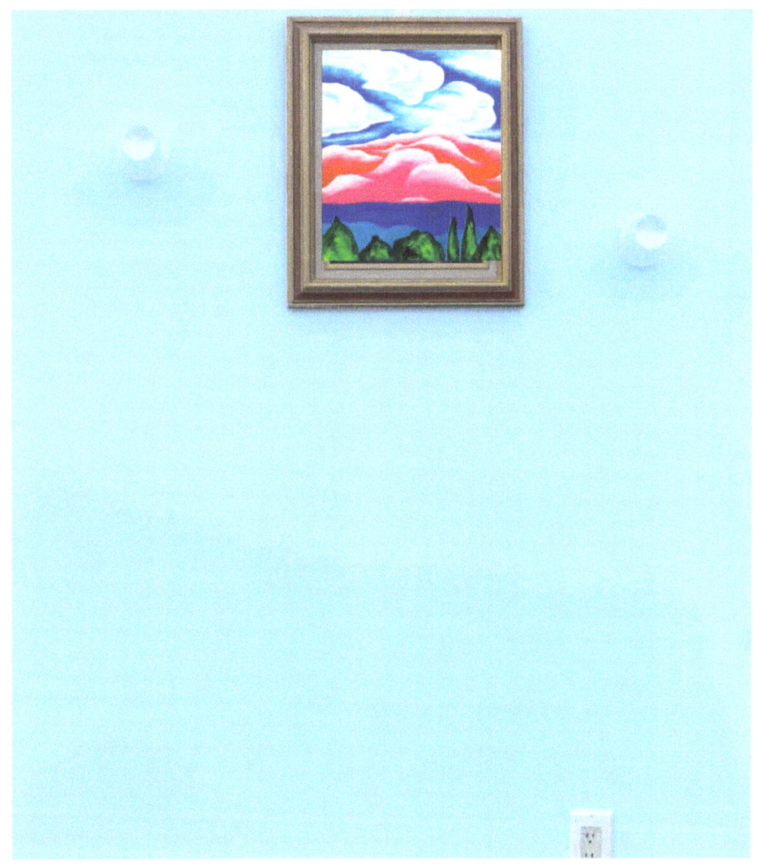

Aurotic Eargasmic
Rory O'Neill
Sound Art, Mixed Media.

Cheap condo… paper thin walls… how well do you know your neighbours?

Roxi Sim Hermsen

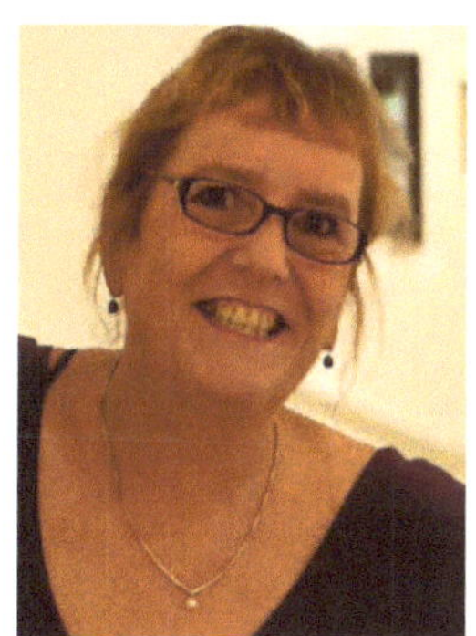

BEd FA Dip. FA 5th year counseling. Vernon based artist Roxi is a real "Culture Vulture and Bohemian at heart. She loves to travel and be inspired by cultural dress, dance and music. Together with Tony her husband of 35 years she has led a creative life as a potter, sculptor, painter, tap dancer and teacher. Roxi is very community oriented helping to found the Salmon Arm Art Gallery, the Salmon Arm Folk music society, the Enderby and District Arts Council, the Okanagan Artisan's guild, the Enderby Wild Wallflower Community Mural Concept and The Okanagan Science Centre. Roxi started painting seriously in 1997 in Grenada W. I., going through 200 ft. of canvas and a suitcase full of paint. Roxi is currently developing healing art workshops and webinars to go with her Pearls of Wisdom Tarot Deck and has recently turned her attention to photography and animation.

www.RoxiArtWork.com

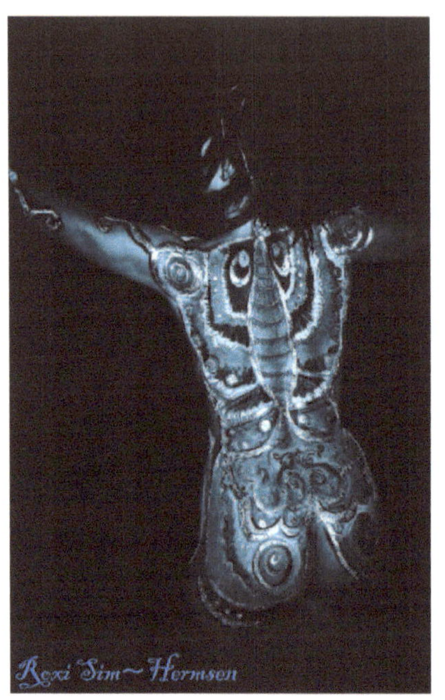

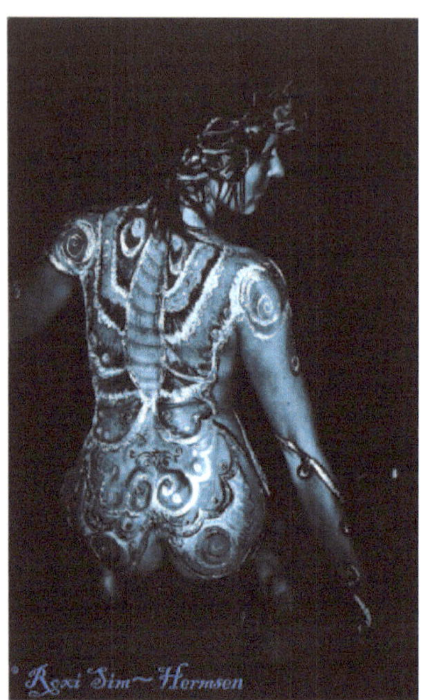

Silver Back to Back Moth 1&2 Diptych
Roxi Sim Hermsen
5x7 each
Photography and body painting

The shimmering silver back moths emerge from the abyss to embrace the darkness.

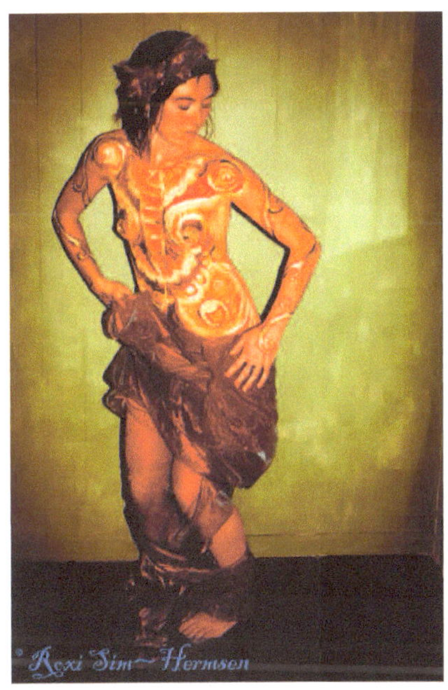

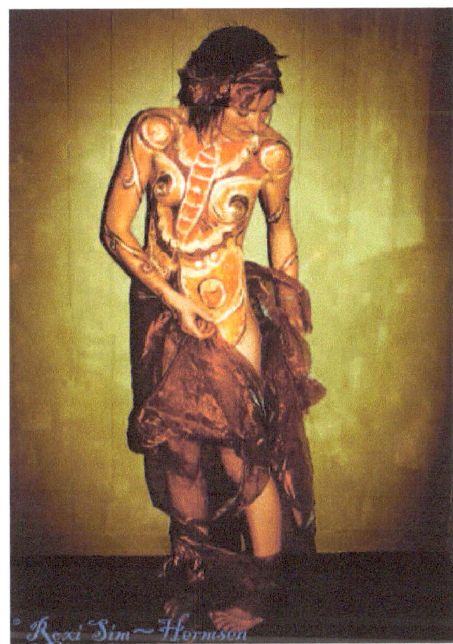

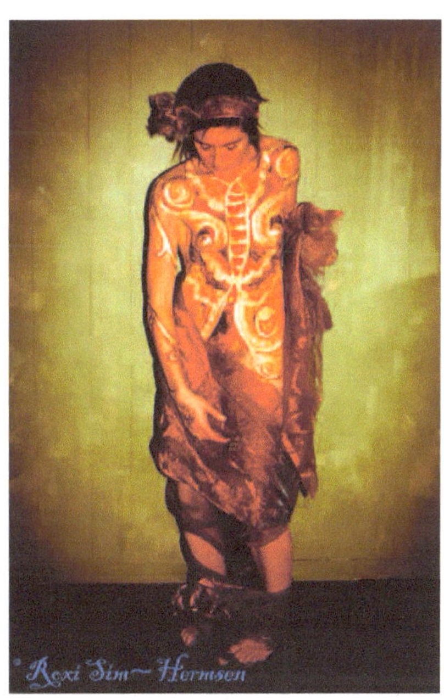

Revealing 1 2 & 3 Triptych
Roxi Sim Hermsen
5x7 each
Photography and body painting

Emerging from her cocoon, the moth slowly reveals
the magical process of metamorphosis and her transformation to the world.

Ryan Robson

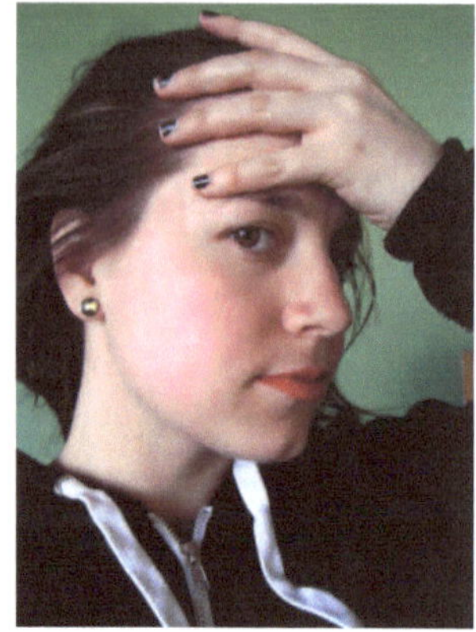

“If everybody says skinny is the only sexy, then why does it feel so good when my thighs rub together. The thicker they are the better it feels.” Ryan gets off by getting down and dirty and she’s always dirty because of all the charcoal. With a fine arts degree from NSCAD University and the position of curator at the Hub Art’s Collective Ryan is passionate about celebrating all things artistic. This show allows her to be free, allows her to let out her sexual side, and encourages her to play with it, play with others and most importantly play with herself. Art is freedom. Let it out!

http://www.TheHubArtsCollective.com/

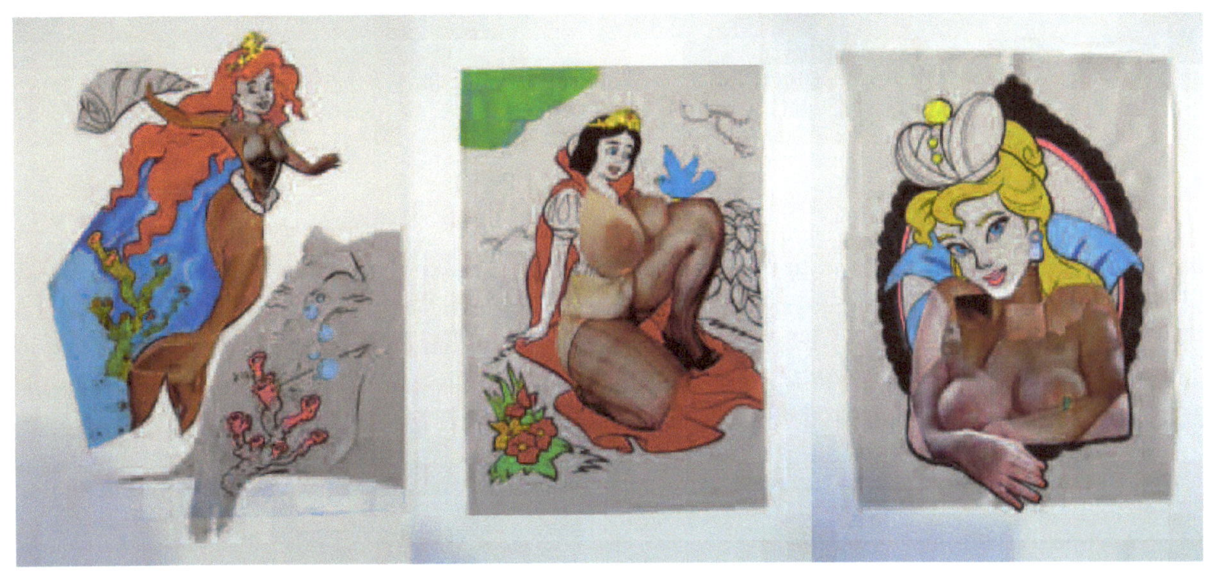

My secret coloring book
Ryan Robson
16x12 each
Collage, acrylic

Growing up in the woods, we played dress up a little different.

Sarah Parsons

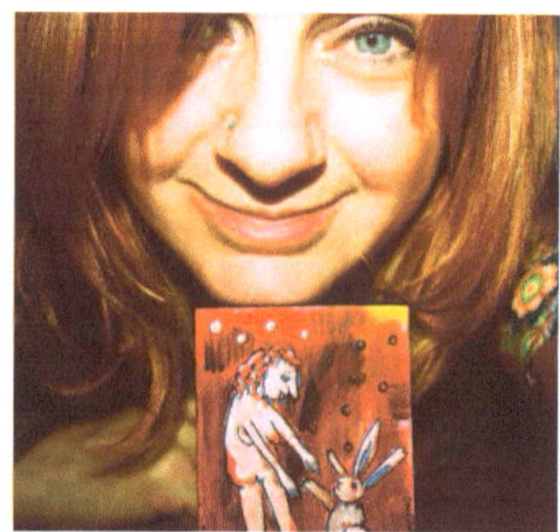

In 2003, Sarah moved from England to the beautiful Okanagan Valley. Sarah, a self taught Artist, has developed her skills over the years and enjoys working in many mediums. Within the past few years, Sarah has been concentrating on her Artistic Career in a more robust fashion, and has enjoyed showing her art at various exhibitions and having her artwork published in several books. Sarah is represented by The New Moon Gallery, West Kelowna, and is currently a resident Artist at the Rotary Centre for the Arts, Kelowna.

www.TheDaySketches.com
www.facebook.com/SarahParsonsArt

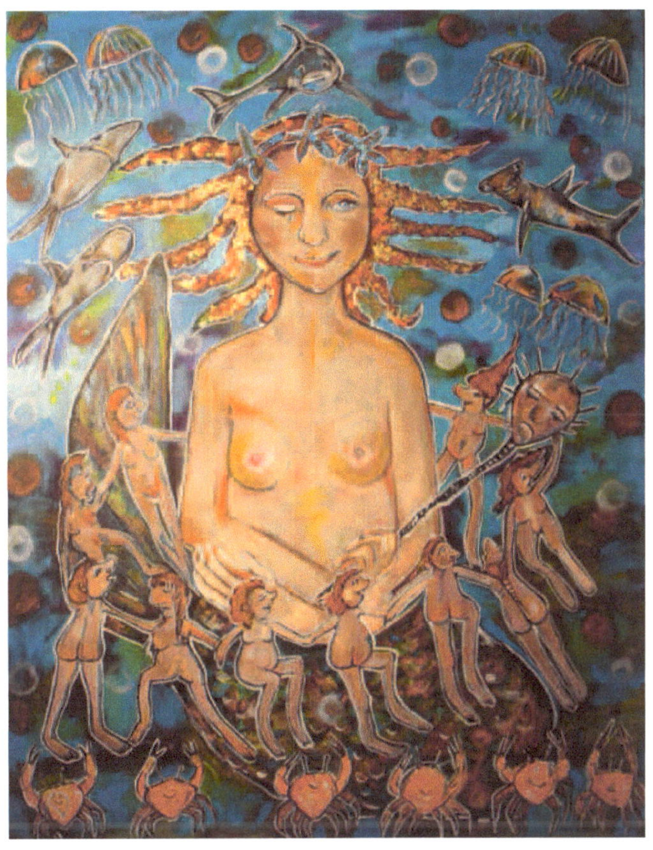

Queen of the Slipstream
Sarah Parsons
29x24
Acrylic and Golf Leaf on Canvas

Captures men to give as sacrifice to the Sea Gods, taking pleasure in keeping a secret souvenir for herself.

Shannon Holand

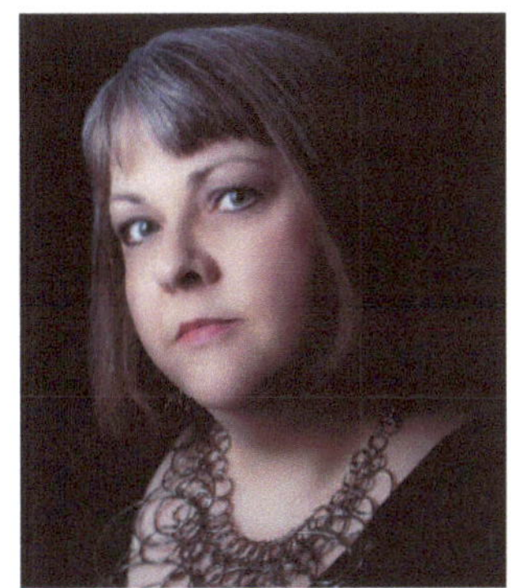

I've been an artist in some form most of my life, but if you had told me 5 years ago I'd be shooting naked people for a living I would have said you were certifiable! Three years ago, this single mom of 18 years became an empty nester and made a long overdue, life altering, career change. An unexpected project had me modeling for a glamour portrait session. Never in a million years did I think I could look THAT sexy as a chunky chick! It was a huge self-esteem boost and ultimately what made me take the plunge to become a professional photographer specializing in intimate artistry and Fractalfotos™. Who knew it was going to be so damn much fun!

www.ShannonHoland.ca

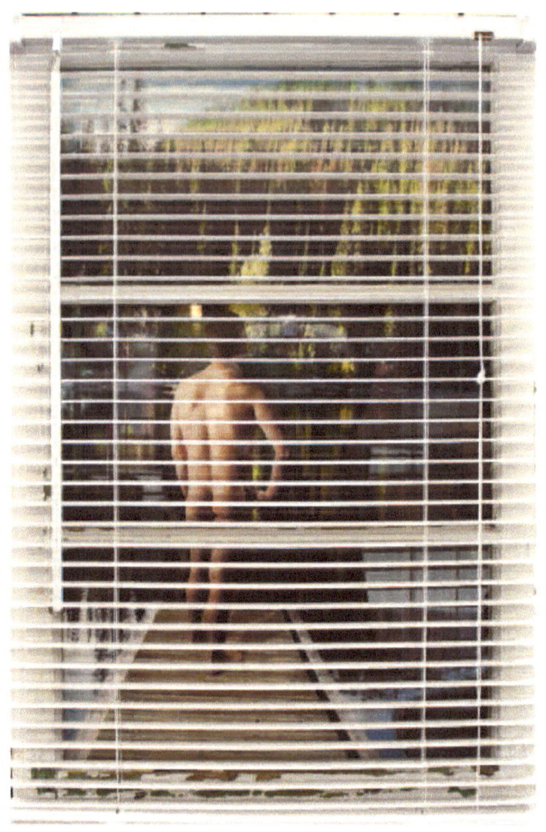

Au Naturel
Shannon Holand
24x36
Canvas print mounted to an old window with a mini blind

Quick, close the blind- grandma's on her way over!

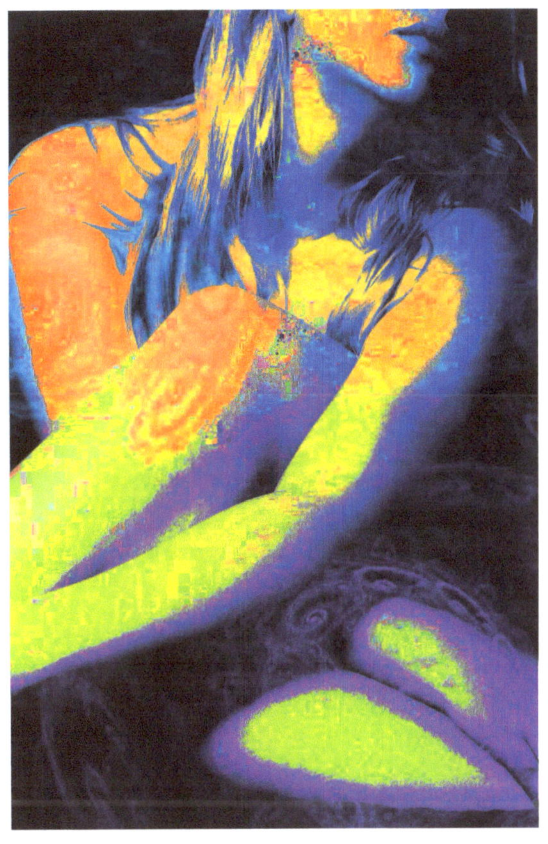

Sexual Synergy
Shannon Holand
16x24
Floating metal Fractalfoto™ print

Fiery Feminine ~ Lustful Lips ~ Titillating Twisted Torso ~
Seductively Sensual ~ Blushing Breasts ~ Arousing Aura … Sexual Synergy!

Sharon Lancaster

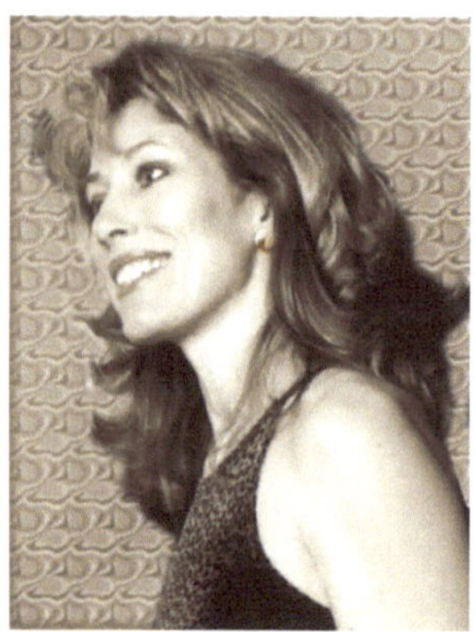

After a half century of searching for home, Sharr relocated to the Okanagan 3 years ago. Penetrating the valley soil with her first roots, stabilizing and revitalizing her eclectic lifestyle. Vibrating with creative and universal energy and intimately connected with the land – Sharr sees beauty and erotica in all of Mother Nature's gifts, resulting in an abundant outpouring of sensual delights. As a writer, teacher, and photographer of life, she challenges her audience – Go Deeper.

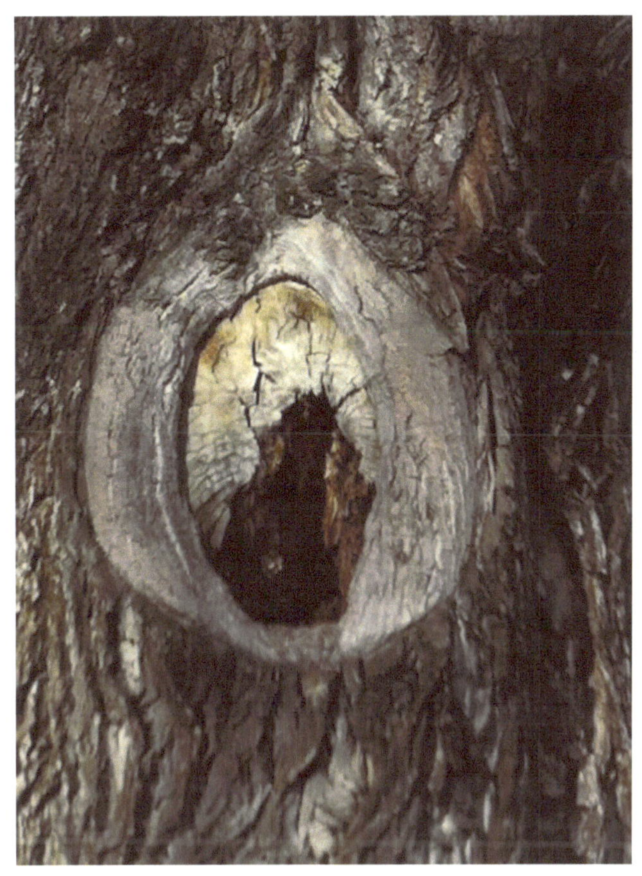

City Park
Sharon Lancaster
16x20
Photograph

A Sanctuary for Wildlife...

Sharon Rose

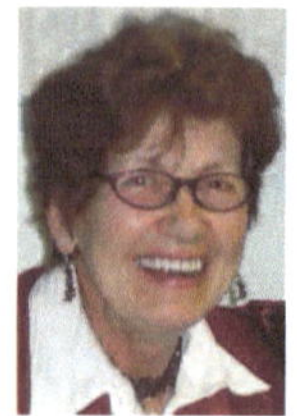

Sharon Rose is co-founder of "Valley Painters" in Merritt, BC where she resided for 22 years. She moved to Vernon in 2002 where she teaches drawing on a part time basis at the Vernon Community Art Centre and is a member of the Livessence Society For Figurative Artists in Kelowna, the Federation of Canadian Artists (FCA) - "Active" status, Kelowna Chapter, and the British Columbia Art Teachers Association (BCATA).

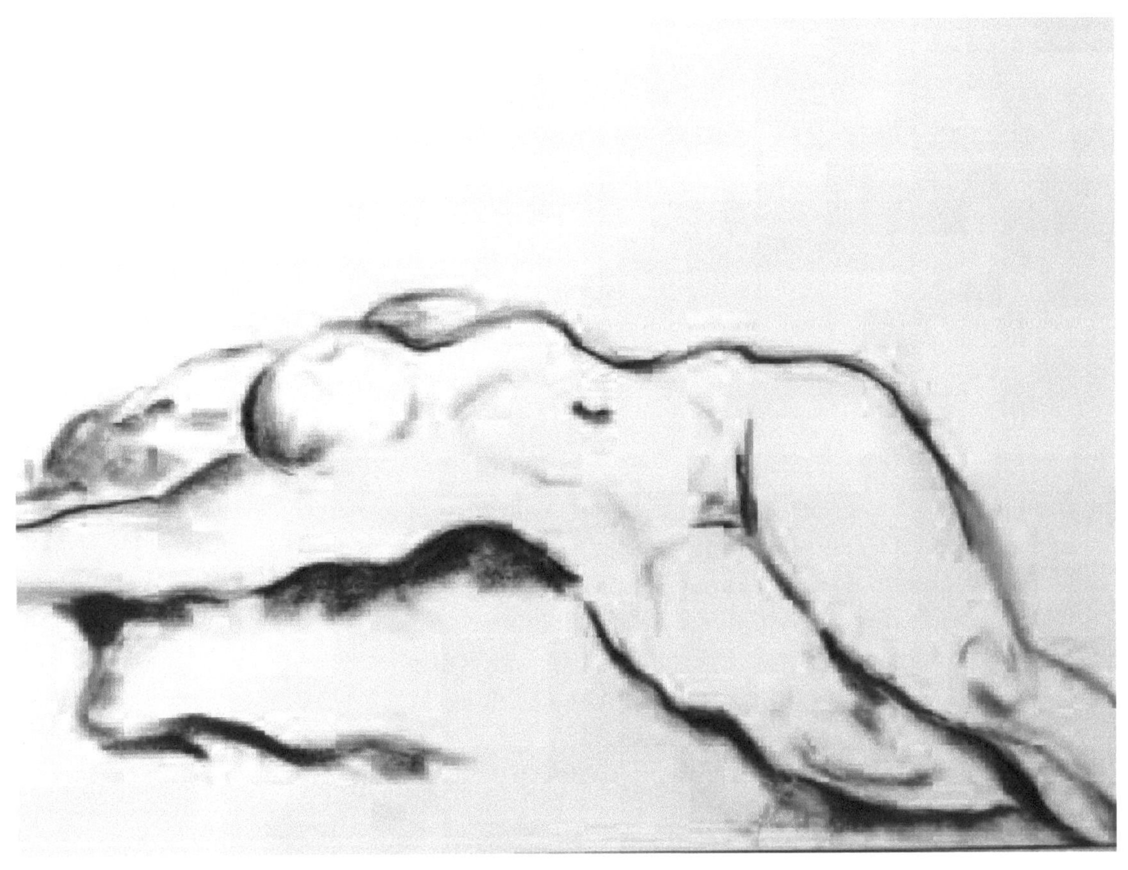

Flow
Sharon Rose
22X28
Vine Charcoal

Though physically still, my inner vision of the model was that of when we permit our mind free reign to play with those images that would never be shared with others.

Shaz

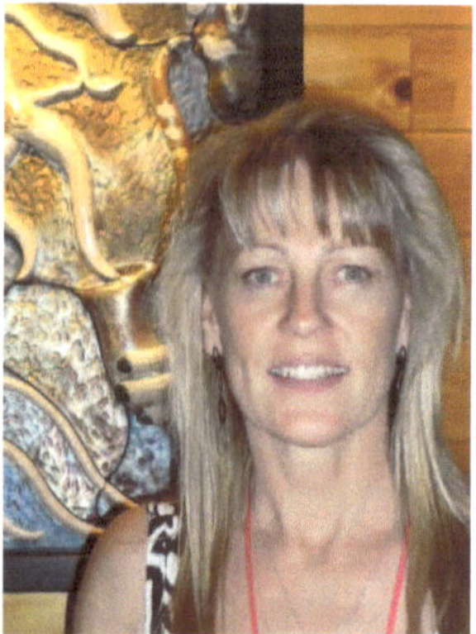

Shaz, a clay artist and stone sculptor, has been creating art in the Okanagan since 1996. Her eclectic interests, energetic personality, and happy disposition are revealed in the diversification and originality of her art. She has an interest in the sensuality of the human body. Living in the Kingdom of Tonga for five years assisted Shaz in expressing the freedom of uninhibited dance and acceptance of self in her art. Music, body, and dance are her inspiration for her current works.

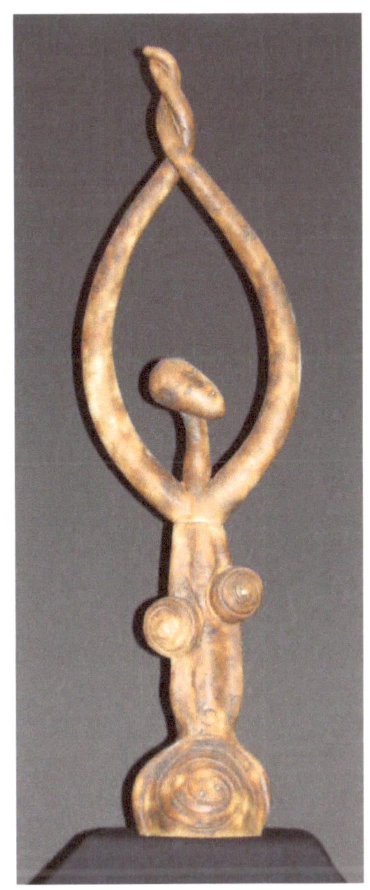

Sunrise
Shaz
28x8x4
Clay

Inner ascent as dawn breaks

Suzanne LeStage

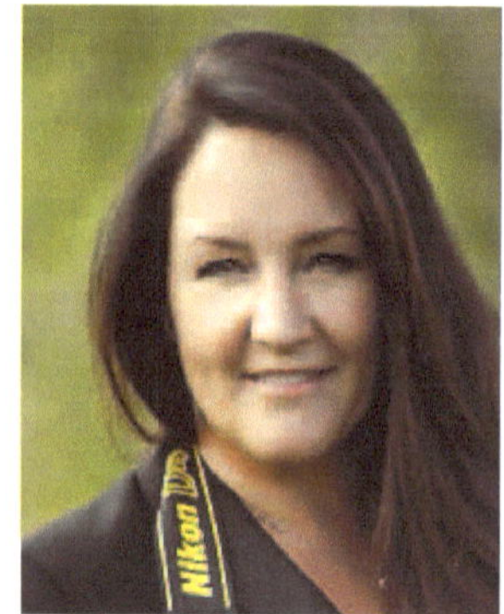

Suzanne childhood was surrounded with Classical music, Art history and hours spend dreaming in the country fields and forests of Vancouver Island. This love of nature, art and music come together with movement, appreciation of light and environment through her creations. This multi-award winning photographer has called the Okanagan home for the past 13 years. Suzanne is available for privately commissioned works internationally.

www.EyesofLestage.com

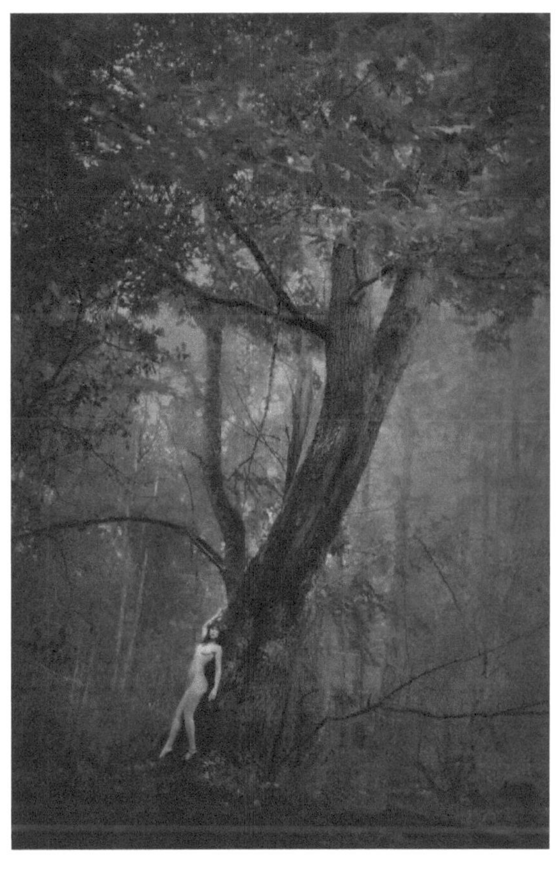

Secret Protector
Suzanne LeStage
20x24
Photography

Celebrating the languid, exotic, sensuality of the elusive forest nymph in a magical forest.

Tina Siddiqui

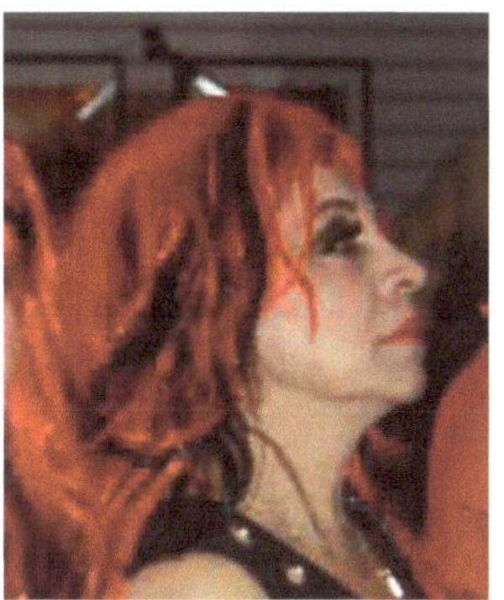

Trained as a Graphic Designer, I paint in a variety of mediums and have participated in group and solo shows here and overseas. Intrigued by the new and unknown is the driving force in my life and this allows me to totally immerse myself in challenging creative endeavours. Rendition of human form is very thrilling for me and I continue to explore newer avenues of expression. Sharing what I have learnt is a joy, hence I teach.

http://fineartamerica.com/profiles/Tina-Siddiqui.html

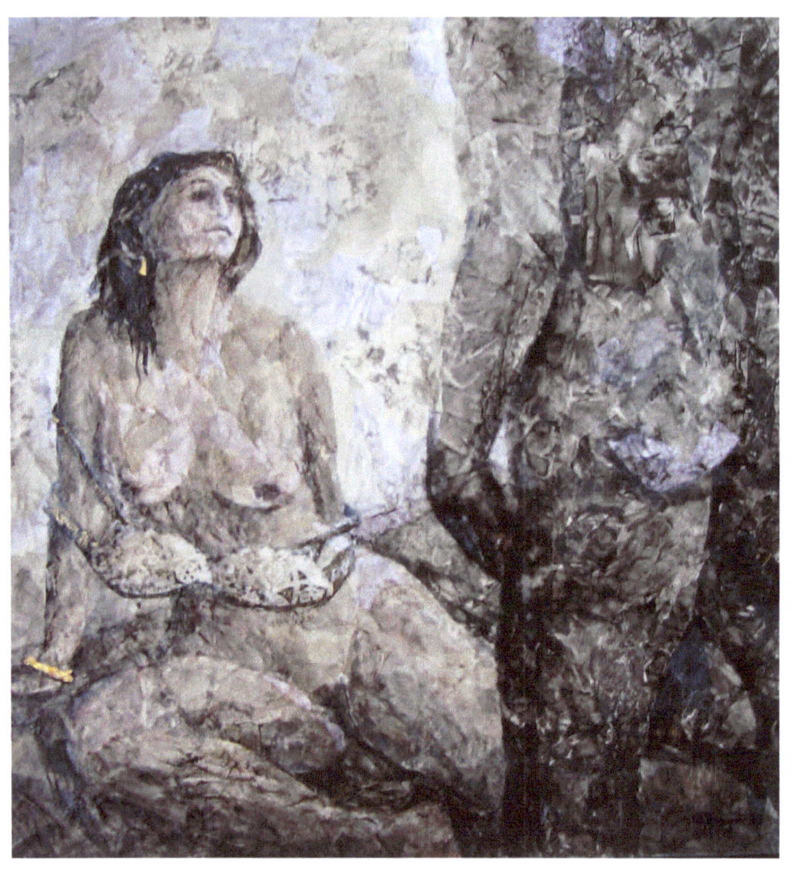

Sweet Surrender
Tina Siddiqui
24x24
Collage on canvas

Sweet surrender during a discreet encounter .... nothing to hold them back.

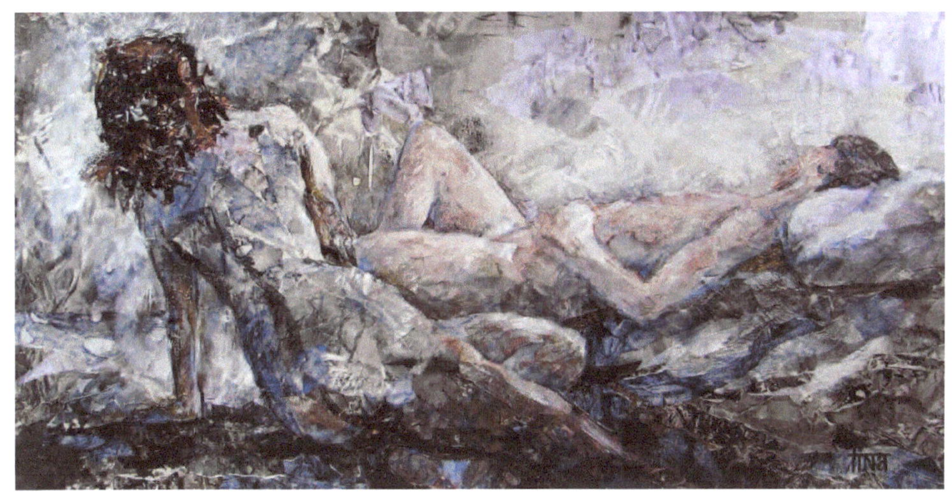

While You Were Sleeping
Tina Siddiqui
24x12
Collage on canvas

She silently ponders, why this strong, magical bond between the keep and the keeper?

Trina Ganson

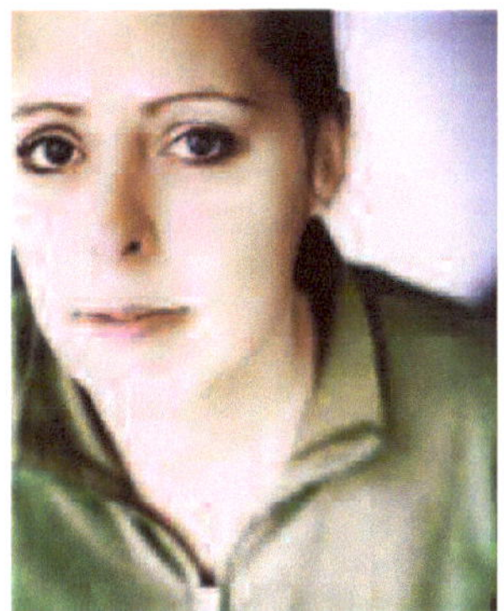

Trina Ganson received her diploma of fine arts from Okanagan University College in 2005. She then became an active member of Malaspina Printmakers Stuido on Granville Island Vancouver. After a number of years Ganson returned to Okanagan to finish her BFA. Trina graduated from the University of British Columbia in 2008, with a BFA majoring in printmaking. Trina Ganson is currently an active member of Studio 113 in the Rotary Centre for the Arts in Kelowna BC.

www.TrinaGanson.wordpress.com

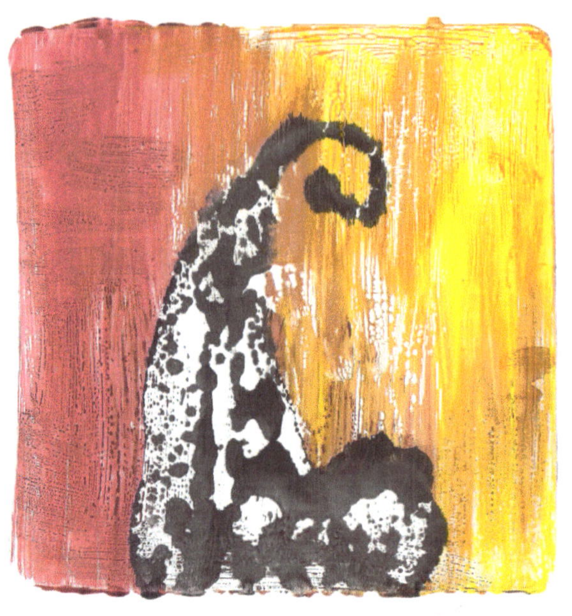

Pear
Trina Ganson
11x14
Monotype

The pear hold it's own secret, on both ends of the scale.

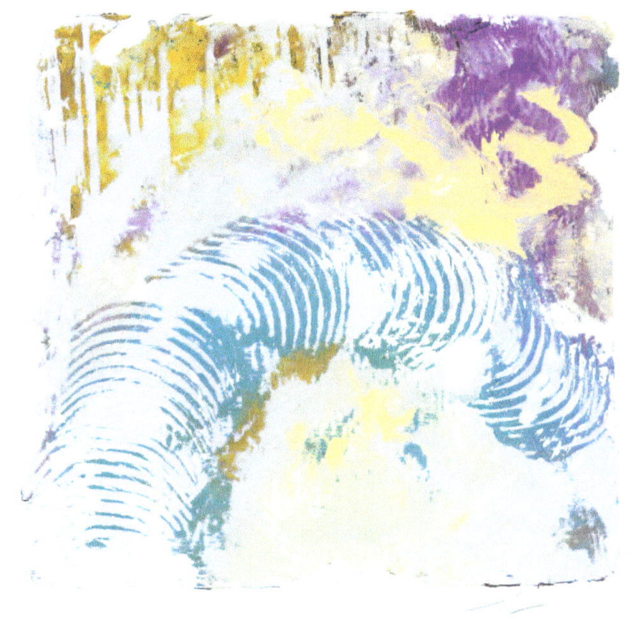

The Toy
Trina Ganson
11x14
Monotype

What most ladies have have and most girls never talk about.

Una Connor, Chad Henderson

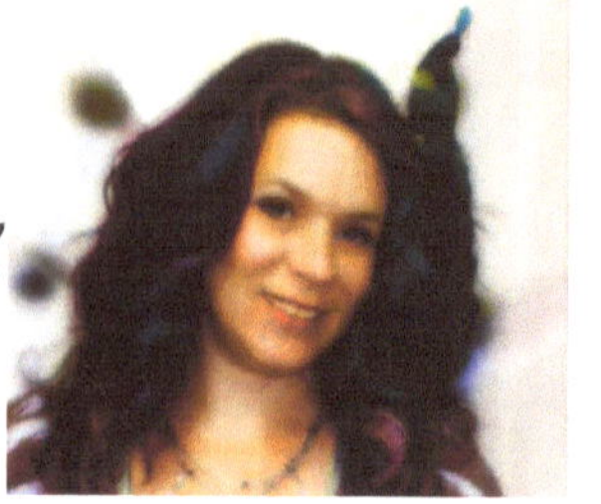

Una, a multi-talented artist, Chad, her inspired husband, married for over a decade, collaborated on this piece over the course of three months. While they were 1000 km. apart through this creative project, technology actually connected them through the distance into a deeper level of intimacy. Una, being the self portrait photographer, while Chad's graphic design makes it all come together for this ultra-sexy, boobielicious photo tile piece.

www.UnaCreations.com

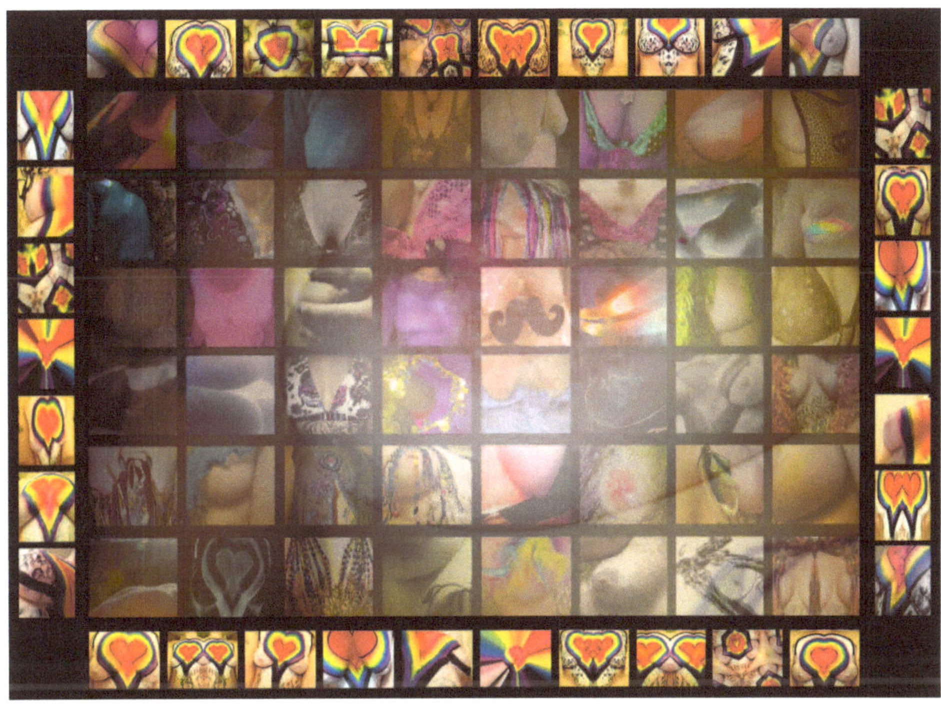

Blatant Obscurity
Una Connor, Chad Henderson
30x20
Photo print on canvas

What's the hubbub 'bout boob?

Victoria Pendragon

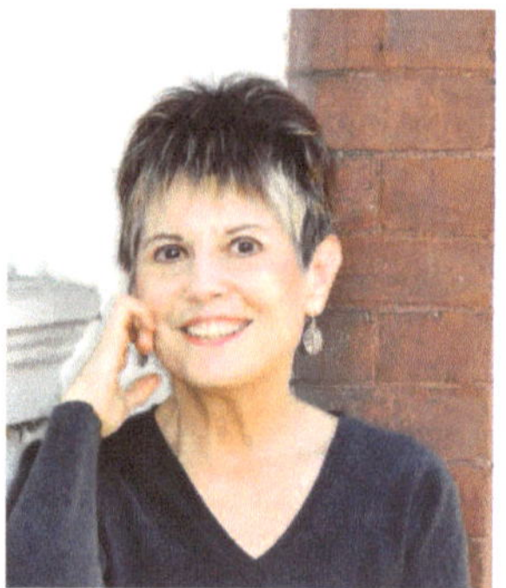

Artist, writer, and former Playboy Bunny, Victoria Pendragon had some of her early erotic stories published by Penthouse Forum but has it found more satisfying work creating small pieces of intimate art for people in love. Inspired by the intense bond with her most recent husband, her Lovers Series captures the energy around intimate connections in an unusual mixed media combination of collage, occasional found objects, and resist dyed silk.

www.VictoriaPendragon.com
www.VictoriaPendragon.artspan.com

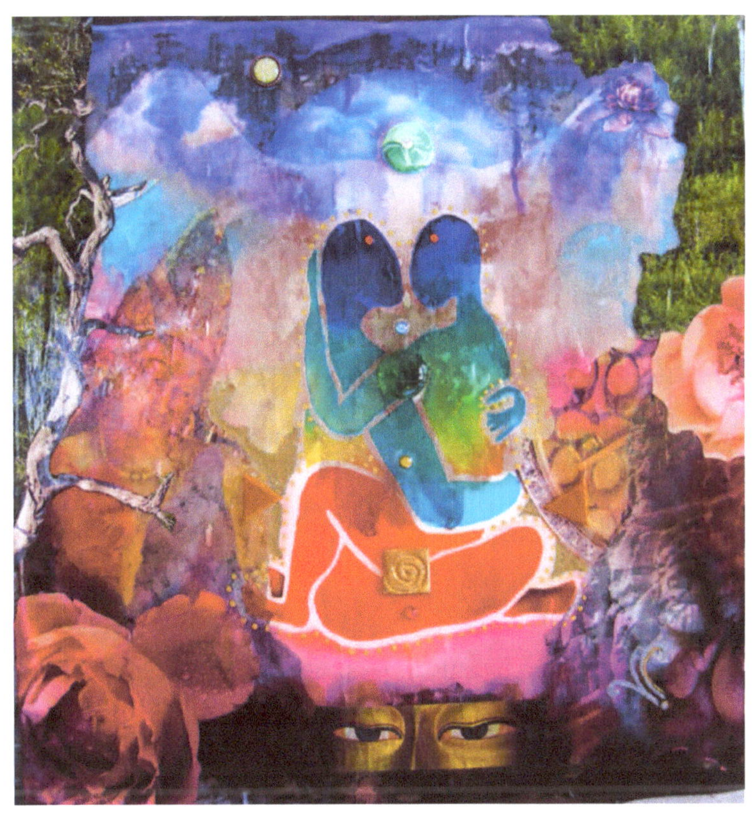

Tantric Comfort
Victoria Pendragon
15x15
Mixed Media/Collage/Resist Dyed Silk

Touching you, touching me.

Victoria Skofteby

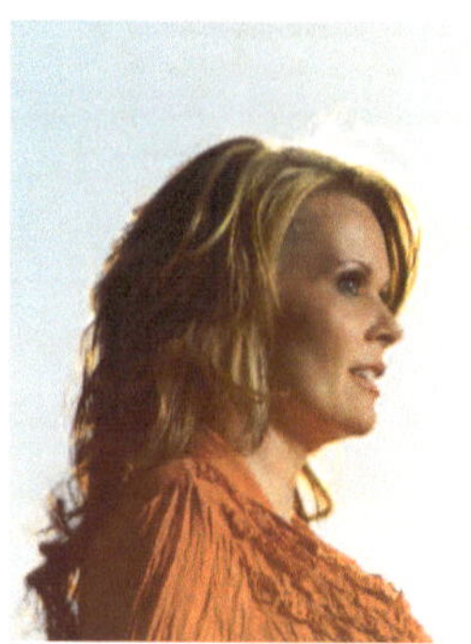

I am a self taught visual artist living in Tappen, B.C. 20 years ago I received a camera as a gift. Since then it has become my third eye. I see beauty in all that surrounds me. I want to capture that beauty and share it with the world. Photography allows me to express my passion and create art. My camera is the portal to my soul.

www.VictoriaSkofteby.com

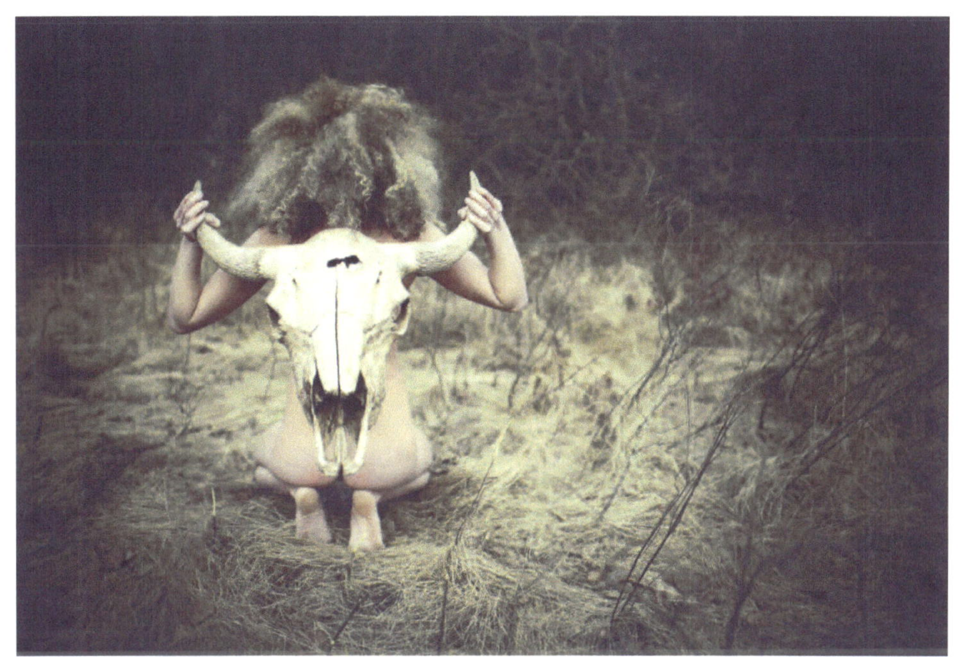

Carnal Desires
Victoria Skofteby
16x24
Photography on Canvas

The sensation of touch sends pulses of pleasure down her spine.

Opening Night

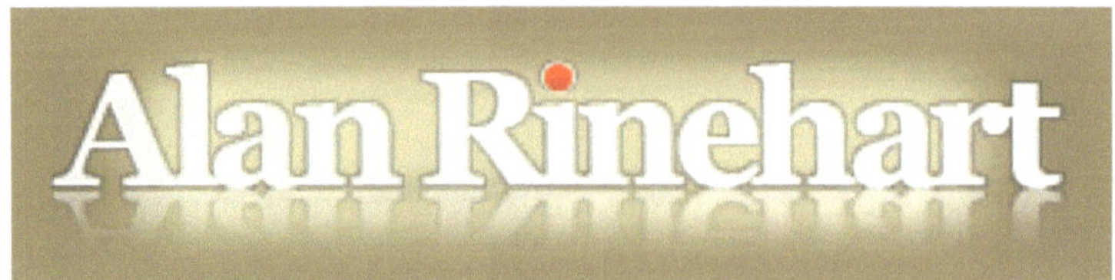

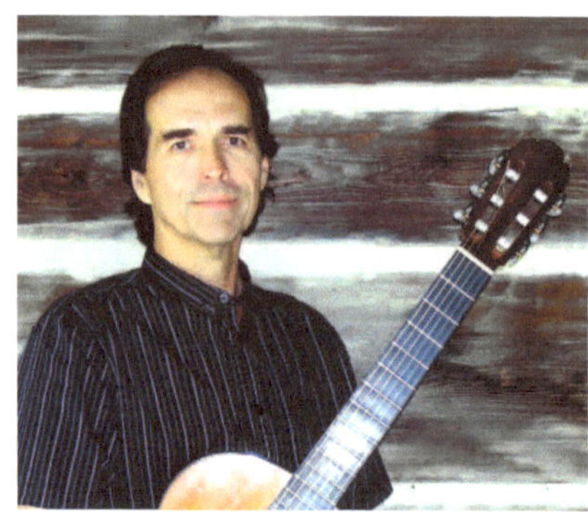

"all the allure one could ask"
The Times of London

Alan Rinehart has made many contributions to the guitar world as a performer, teacher, and music editor. Completing studies at Western Michigan University and a Professional Music Training Diploma from Vancouver Community College, he studied lute repertoire and technique in London, England at the Early Music Centre with Anthony Rooley, Jakob Lindberg, Nigel North and Emma Kirkby.

"The playing was consistently clean and musical, and he has a pleasantly relaxed manner which won over the audience right from the word go."

GUITAR INTERNATIONAL magazine, London, England, (London Debut, The Purcell Room)

In addition to many concert recitals, he has performed at international music festivals in Spain, the United States, Toronto and Quebec and appeared on CBC radio and TV. He is a co-founder of The Vancouver Guitar Quartet, which became a regular part of the Vancouver and Western Canadian music scene from the late 1980s to 2003, with many concert and radio appearances.

He has released three solo CDs and one CD with the Vancouver Guitar Quartet that have received international critical praise; Renaissance Masters and Latin Romantics in 1981, Musical Banquet in 2000, The Golden Century in 2010 and Estampas with the VGQ in 1999.

"His approach had about it a sensitive and seductive delicacy." The Province, Vancouver B.C.

From 1983 to 2003 he was a faculty member of the music schools at the University of British Columbia and Vancouver Community College. He currently lives in Kelowna, BC

www.AlanRinehart.com

theatre86

the·a·tre eight·y·six [thee-uh-ter ey-tee siks]

noun

- a non-profit troupe of independent artists motivated by a passion for the arts

verb

- to see the talent, to learn the talent, to be the talent
- to elevate the community's awareness of the arts through various mediums and expressions of art
- to reinforce the relationship of the artist and the community by bringing the arts directly to the people rather than only waiting for the audience to come to the arts
- to uphold the values of community, art, knowledge, opinions, ideas, expression and creation

Jessika LaFramboise, an artist showing visual work, will also be performing a 10-15 minute X-rated monologue called "Slut", and we will all be surprised on the evening. I have no doubt it will be fun, and I am looking forward to it!

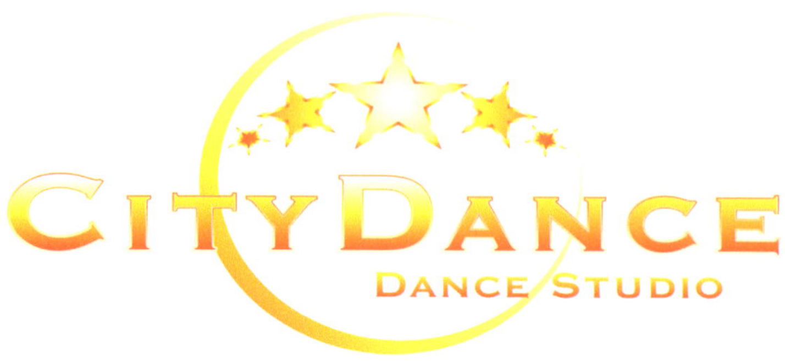

"City Dance is one year old an we could not be more pleased by the reception we've had from our students and the community. Our goal was to create not only a place to learn to dance, but an environment that nurtures our students in a way that other studios do not. Our students quickly become a part of our dance family and, in addition to the lessons, dancers congregate on Friday nights for our practice dances and special occasions which are open to everyone whether they are students or not. True to our dreams, the studio has become a place to learn, have fun and socialize.

We specialize in ballroom, latin, swing dancing, HipHop and children's ballet and jazz as well as Zumba. We have private and group lessons available. Every Friday night at 8pm we have open dances. Everyone is welcome.

If you are interested in learning more about our studio and our group and private lessons packages, please contact us at the studio at 250-307-4955 or email us at info@citydanceok.com"

The Argentine Tango:

"Argentine Tango has been described in many different ways. Some take a tongue-in-cheek approach and call it "the vertical expression of horizontal desire." Others view the dance as a physical expression of the pain, the passion, and the life of a people. In this way, it can be used as a non-verbal language, to express one's self in new ways. I've often heard tango described as a wonder drug that makes you younger, sexier, and more of who you really are, while others shrug their shoulders and say simply, "It's a way of life." The response of a philosopher.

Somehow that simplicity lends itself to layer upon layer of meaning. Yearning, desire, escape. Each person brings their own light and darkness with them, and each looks to finds their place in tango. And we all work to make our peace with the dance. It may be a constant struggle. Like any good fight, though, it's worth it. There are moments of transcendence, of desire fulfilled, of finding oneself lost in another's arms. That's the power of this dance."

The Paso Doble:

"It is full of energy, strict and powerful. With his haughty, bold pride the dancer expresses his superiority like a Torero. He convincingly transfers this solemn appeal to the audience. The woman, on the other hand, generates a self-confident distance to him, without surrendering to the power of the master. She is the literal image of the "Capa"; the red cloth that the Torero uses to keep the bull under control, and is, like this, lithe, agile and elegant."

MUSARTIQA

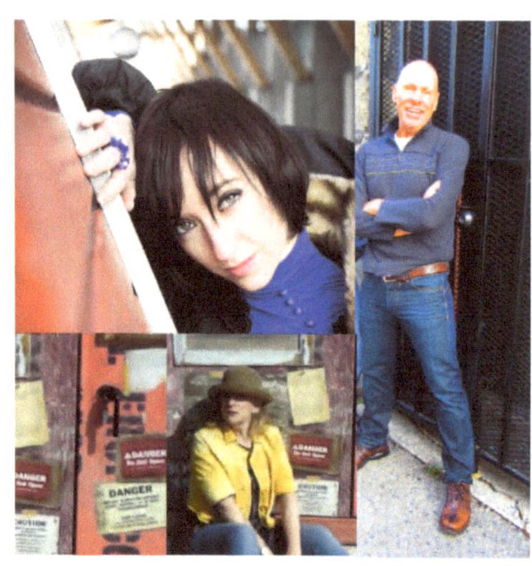

MUSARTIQA is a combination of music, art and dance.

It is a synergy of 3 different artists and their individual disciplines. The sensual movements of Dancer Angel Jutzi to the pulsating rhythm of the keyboard or the arousing sound of the saxophone of multi instrumentalist Tony Koenen while Angela Bonten captures the moment with the subtle and erotic movement of the brush. What secrets do these performers hold? Will they subtly be revealed through their art?

Angela Bonten

Angela Bonten is a mixed- media Kelowna artist who has exhibited extensively. As a graduate of the fine art and fibre art program of Grant MacEwan University College, her work often contains textiles combined with painting. She describes herself as a mark maker, using whatever tool it takes to leave an artistic mark. Angela is always experimenting with her medium and is an out of the box thinker! Her studio is located at the Rotary Centre for the arts. In her paintings you will find many different layers often with hidden messages. Eccentric and vibrant, she is a mysterious keeper of secrets, to only be shared by some!

www.AngelaBonten.com

Angel Jutzi

Angel Jutzi began dancing at the age of three and continued her studies at The National Ballet School of Canada. Angel went on to train at Ryerson University before being accepted into the Mentorship Program with Ballet BC. Angel was offered a contract with Ballet Kelowna where she danced for four seasons, during that time she spent two summers attending the Banff Professional Dance Program. Angel has performed many original works both in Canada and internationally. In 2009 she was honoured to premiere the Atonement program at the 13th Annual Bangkok International Dance Festival with “MOVE: the company” under the direction of Joshua Beamish. Angel is the founding Artistic director of Zebra Eyes Contemporary Dance in Kelowna.

www.ZebraEyesDance.com

Tony Koenen

Tony Koenen is a Canadian Singer, song writer and multi-instrumentalist with an international accredited top twenty European hit “Dear Santa” produced by George Blondheim. His passion is creating messages through music. Some logical and understandable, some secretive and metaphorically twisted. Improvisation is a musical form Koenen loves to explore. “Musartiqa” allows him an uncharted, unscripted, unrehearsed musical Journey that even he, at times, is unsure of what will transpire and evolve. Always edgy, always fresh, Koenen has a large library of original works that have been recorded by many artists and is always exploring new musical avenues.

www.TonyKoenenMusic.com

Yann Andre

Event Photographer

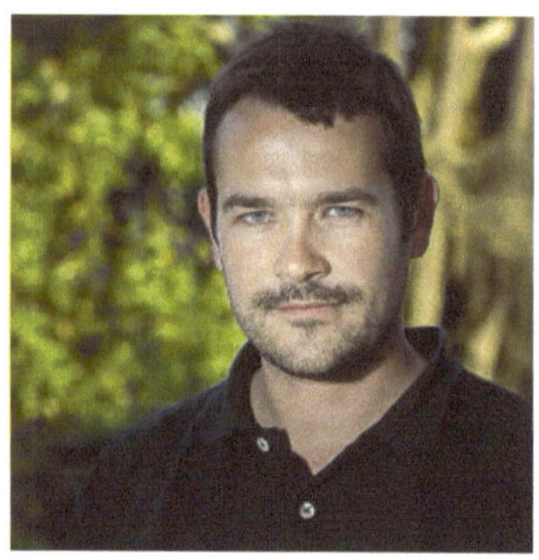

Yann Andre is a very talented, local, emerging photographer. He moved to the Okanagan from France in 2010. He is working on his PhD in Chemistry and devotes much of his free time on photographic pursuits. He loves to create beautiful images and especially enjoys photographing people, landscapes and wildlife. He is also skilled in custom printing and matting of photographic images, and has helped other photographers prepare their work for exhibition.

Yann has earned an impressive number of photographic awards and honourable mentions for his images. His work has been displayed in several local expositions. He has had his images selected to compete at a national level with the Canadian Association of Photographic Artists. Most recently (June 2013) at the Central Okanagan Photographic Society's annual awards banquet he was the winner of three trophies for photographic images and achievements in 2012/13.

Yann is well on his way to becoming an accomplished photographer/artist.

An event photographer was requested via the Central Okanagan Photographic Society's Facebook group, and Yann stepped up. He will be photographing guests as they arrive, and also take candid shots throughout the evening.

These images will be available for free guest download from the Okanagan Erotic Art Show website, http://www.OkanaganEroticArtShow.com, and he will also provide images available for printing directly for a small cost. Here is a sample photograph of his work:

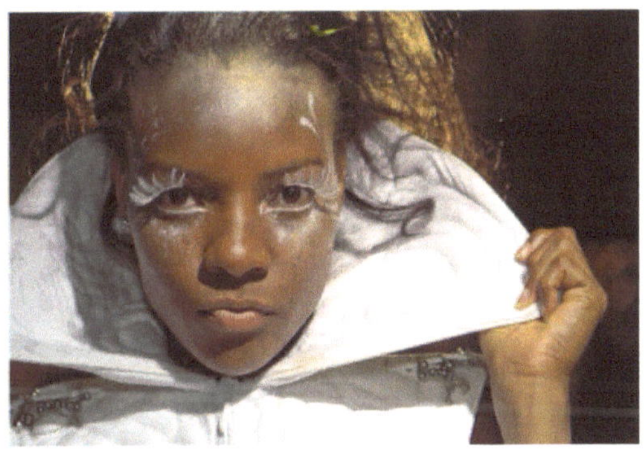

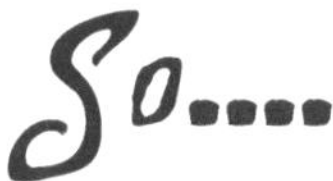

There you have it. Another year for the Okanagan Erotic Show is complete.

All the works submitted are a result of many artists' work, labours of love, labours of intensity, each one a love affair with that artist, each one had merits of whether to be included. As the artist determines which stroke stays on the canvas, so too, did the jury have the requirement to determine which artwork would be shown this year. The jurying was difficult but necessary.   Thank you to everyone who entered, I hope you will enter again next year.

I don't pretend to be a professional publisher or writer, but I do make a huge effort to acknowledge artists who participate in my shows. One way I do that is by the web site, another way is by the catalog. Catalogs give substantiation and solidity to an artist's work by saying it is important enough to be printed. I have the skills, and the knowledge, so why not... ?

All participating artists have the option and choice to be in the catalog, and they do not pay for inclusion. Being in this catalog is not a requirement for being in the show.

I am quite thorough on the FAQ page on the website, and many questions repeat themselves every year. Please consider in sending in a submission, share the Call with your friends. Maybe see you next year.

Julia Trops

http://www.OkanaganEroticArtShow.com
http://www.Facebook.com/EroticArtShow
http://www.SparklingHill.com
http://www.facebook.com/SparklingHill

www.ingramcontent.com/pod-product-compliance
Lightning Source LLC
LaVergne TN
LVHW070119110826
845147LV00002B/155